Open Kitchen

GREAT BRITISH CHEFS

Left: Angel Zapata Martin
uses tweezers to garnish his
onion and anchovy tart with
edible flowers.

Open Kitchen

There's something unquestionably alluring about a restaurant kitchen. Typically hidden from diners' eyes, it's where raw ingredients are transformed into something spectacular, through processes virtually inconceivable to the home cook. The new-found flavours and textures on the plate are often the only insight into the expertise at play behind the pass.

When a restaurant experience blows us away, we find ourselves wanting to know more about the person behind the food. Chefs often endure gruelling journeys to success, so how did they do it? Where do they find inspiration? What is the creative process powering their signature style? Answering these questions was the reason Great British Chefs was founded in 2010 – to remove the disconnect between the home cook and professional, looking deeper into the country's finest culinary minds.

Over the past decade, the UK's restaurant scene has changed immeasurably. Chefs are now focused on sustainability and quality of produce; provenance, sourcing, foraging and food miles are all familiar terms. The UK has one of the most diverse and exciting culinary scenes in the world, with top quality food coming from street food vans, seaside cafés, country pubs or Michelin-starred restaurants. The lines between casual and fine dining are increasingly blurred.

Join us, then, as we peel back the curtain on some of the most exciting UK kitchens. Open Kitchen was born out of a desire to lay bare our variety of talent, while also providing insight into the craft of professional cookery. Over the past year, we visited as many top chefs' restaurants as possible, to capture first-hand the inner workings of their kitchens. We collected a total of fifty recipes from thirty chefs, demonstrating their signature styles and culinary ethos; all of them are exclusive to this book.

What follows is, of course, just a snapshot of the UK's current food scene but it's one that we feel represents the range of cuisines, kitchens and approaches to cookery showcased throughout the UK right now. From the Malaysian street food of Abby Lee and the traditional Japanese cookery of Shuko Oda, to the ultra-refined Michelin-starred dishes of Simon Rogan and Lisa Goodwin-Allen, each recipe helps to paint a picture of our culinary landscape in 2023. Dishes range from simple snacks that come together in an under an hour, to complex, multi-element constructions that will require some planning and ambition.

It's been nothing but a pleasure creating this book and we're immensely proud of our ever-evolving restaurant scene. It's our hope that, as you flick through these pages and attempt some of the recipes for yourself, you'll feel as if you're getting a glimpse into a different, often secretive, world. A huge thank you to all the chefs who helped us get closer to the magic.

Left: Koya founder Shuko Oda spreads out steamed rice to form the base of her dish chirashi zushi with candied herring, golden beetroot and monk's beard. Next spread: Simon Rogan picks micro leaves from his polytunnels in Cartmel, which are used to garnish dishes at his three Michelin-starred restaurant, L'Enclume.

A true champion of Scotland's natural larder, Roberta Hall-McCarron first opened Edinburgh's Little Chartroom in 2018, having honed her craft working under Tom Kitchin. By 2021, the restaurant's popularity had forced her and her husband-cum-business partner Shaun to relocate to a larger site while they transformed the old space into their second restaurant and wine bar, Eleanore. Roberta's bold, seasonal food sees her bring unique twists to classic flavour combinations, with a distinct focus on Scottish produce and simple yet refined presentation, and continues to prove a hit both with Edinburgh locals and those visiting from further afield.

Roberta Hall-McCarron

Below: Roberta uses tweezers to top the blistered skin of her barbecued mackerel with smoked almonds and delicate micro herbs.

Above: since changing location in 2021, Roberta's restaurant The Little Chartroom has been centred around an impressive open kitchen.

Serves 6

1 hour 30 minutes, plus time for the barbecue to heat up
Equipment: Barbecue or griddle pan, blender

Mackerel

6 fresh mackerel, filleted, bones and membrane removed
18 cherry tomatoes, halved
50g caster sugar
18 smoked almonds, roughly chopped
1 handful micro cress

Basil and almond sauce

100g fresh basil
60g spinach
150g almond milk
40g smoked almonds
30g rapeseed oil
1 lemon, juiced
ice water, as needed

Barbecued mackerel

This simple mackerel recipe involves cooking the fish on a barbecue or griddle pan to achieve a slightly charred, crispy skin. Roberta suggests leaving the mackerel uncovered in the fridge for a day before cooking to allow the skin to dry out slightly. Served with a bright basil and smoked almond sauce and a garnish of roasted cherry tomatoes, it makes a summery starter or light main course.

Tomatoes Preheat the oven to 70°C and prepare a barbecue for cooking the mackerel, if using.

Sprinkle the cherry tomatoes with 50g sea salt and the sugar, then leave them at room temperature for 30 minutes on an oven tray.

After 30 minutes, roast the cherry tomatoes for 30 minutes to 1 hour. You want them to have broken down and softened a little. Remove from the oven and set aside.

Basil and almond sauce Bring a large pot of water to a boil and prepare a large bowl of ice water. Add the spinach and basil to the boiling water and blanch for a few seconds until the leaves just begin to wilt. Remove the leaves with a slotted spoon then transfer to the ice bath. Once cold, squeeze out all the water.

Transfer the basil, spinach, almond milk and smoked almonds to a blender and blitz until smooth, then gradually add the oil before blending. Add salt to taste and set aside – the lemon juice is added just before serving.

Mackerel Lightly oil the mackerel and season with salt on both sides. If using a griddle pan, heat it to a medium heat. Add the mackerel skin side down for 1-2 minutes. Carefully flip the fillets over and cook for a few seconds more, then transfer to a serving plate.

To serve Garnish the mackerel with the chopped smoked almonds, cherry tomatoes and micro cress. Add the lemon juice to the basil and almond sauce, then pour next to the fish.

Serves 6
2 hours 30 minutes,
plus setting time
Equipment: 6 panna cotta
moulds, roughly 8 cm in diameter
and 4 cm tall

Panna cotta
240g barley
250g double cream
250g whole milk
35g caster sugar
8g bronze leaf gelatin

Berry soup
500g frozen mixed berries
150g caster sugar

To serve
30g buckwheat
90g raspberries, halved
150g strawberries, roughly chopped
150g blueberries, halved
white balsamic vinegar, to taste
20 oxalis leaves
10g bee pollen

Toasted barley panna cotta

Toasted barley may not be a flavour typically associated with desserts but here Roberta uses it to flavour a panna cotta, which is garnished with an assortment of summer berries and buckwheat. She also uses a touch of vinegar to balance out the sweetness. If you don't have moulds, you can also make and serve the panna cotta in glasses or bowls.

Panna cotta Add the barley to a dry frying pan and toast over medium heat until golden brown. It needs to be heavily toasted but not burnt, so keep an eye on it and move it regularly. Transfer to a bowl to cool.

Add the cream, milk and sugar to a pan with the cooled barley. Heat the mixture but don't let it boil, and infuse the barley for 20 minutes. Meanwhile, bloom the gelatin in cold water.

Strain the cream mixture through a sieve. Squeeze out any excess liquid from the gelatin, and add it into the warm cream mixture. Stir until the gelatin is completely dissolved, then pour the panna cotta mixture into the moulds. They should each hold about 90g of mixture.

Place the panna cotta into the fridge to set for 3 hours.

Berry soup Mix the frozen berries and sugar together in a heatproof bowl and set aside, covered.

Bring a pan of water to the boil, then turn the heat down to low. Place the berries over the pan and cook for 2 hours. All the juices should come out of the berries as the fruit steams. Check the water level in the pan regularly, topping up with boiling water as needed.

After 2 hours, strain the berry juice through a sieve, and transfer to a container. Chill until cold.

To serve Toast the buckwheat over a low heat in a dry pan, stirring frequently, until fragrant. Set aside.

Mix the fresh fruit with a few spoonfuls of the berry soup, and a small dash of white balsamic – just enough to balance out the sweetness.

To remove the panna cotta from the mould, gently dip it into warm water for a few seconds then place the plate you are going to serve the panna cotta on top of the mould. Flip it over, then remove the mould. If the panna cotta gets stuck, just dip the mould in warm water again.

Dress the panna cotta with the berries on one side, and sprinkle the buckwheat over the berry soup-soaked fresh fruit. Garnish with oxalis and bee pollen.

It was a culinary tour of China and its ancient traditions and culture that first gave Andrew the understanding and drive that have been the bedrock of his career. He returned to London inspired, opening A. Wong in 2012, where Andrew now celebrates regional Chinese cooking, whilst marrying his fine dining training with influences from his London upbringing and Chinese heritage. The menus at A. Wong take diners on a gastronomic journey across China, paying homage to centuries of technique and tradition, with Andrew's cultural appreciation, creative flair and talent shifting perceptions of Chinese food in the UK and winning him two Michelin stars in the process.

Andrew Wong

Below: Spices such as cassia bark, cinnamon sticks and black peppercorns are wok-fried in oil until fragrant.

Right: Andrew opened A. Wong in the same Pimlico location as his parents' former Cantonese restaurant.

Right: Andrew wraps his spices for poaching his soy chicken in muslin, to keep them all together.

Serves 4 as a side dish
30 minutes
Equipment: Wok, spice grinder

Seasoning powder
10g dried chillies
3g Sichuan peppercorns
100ml vegetable oil

Tofu
400g medium set tofu, diced into
2 cm cubes
50g high-fat beef mince
5g doubanjiang
10g hot pot paste
20g chopped Sichuanese pickled
chillies or Tantan Xiang chillies
15g ginger, minced
3g fermented black beans
10g Shaoxing wine
2g sugar
1g ground white pepper
2g oyster sauce
10g of potato starch mixed with
20g water into a slurry

To serve
1 spring onion, finely chopped
2g sesame oil
sesame seeds, for garnish

Mapo tofu

Andrew Wong's recipe for this classic Sichuanese dish is deeply savoury and spicy. It layers different fermented ingredients like doubanjiang, black beans and pickled chillies and finishes with a dusting of crispy fried chilli and tingly Sichuan peppercorns. Despite the strong, punchy flavours, tofu is still the star of the show, gently slipped in during the last five minutes to preserve its delicate texture.

Seasoning powder Heat the oil in a pan to 150°C. Add the chillies and peppercorns and fry until fragrant and lightly toasted. Carefully drain off the oil, and let the spices cool for 5 minutes. Grind the fried chillies and peppercorns into a powder and set aside.

Tofu and beef Blanch the tofu in boiling water for 30 seconds, then drain and chill in cold water.

Fry the beef in a wok until the fat begins to render. Add the doubanjiang and hot pot paste and fry until the oil turns red. Add the pickled chillies, ginger and black beans, then mix. Deglaze the pan with Shaoxing wine.

Add 200ml water and bring to a simmer, then add the oyster sauce, sugar and white pepper. Taste and add salt if needed. Add the tofu to the pan and simmer for 5 minutes. Add half the potato starch slurry then cook for a few minutes – if it doesn't quite thicken enough, add the rest of the slurry.

To serve Garnish with sesame seeds, sesame oil, chopped spring onion and the seasoning powder. Serve with steamed jasmine rice.

Serves 4
3 hours
Equipment: Pastry brush, meat hook

1.6kg chicken
20g maltose syrup, warmed slightly
2 tsp sesame oil

Poaching liquor
150g ginger, thinly sliced
oil, for cooking
75g spring onion
2-3 litres light soy sauce
80g dark soy sauce
750g rock sugar
28g red yeast rice
28g salt
35g coriander
1 star anise
1 bay leaf
1 cinnamon stick
2 cardamom pod
½ teaspoon fennel seeds
1 piece cassia bark
grating of nutmeg
a few black peppercorns
a few Sichuan peppercorns
½ teaspoon cumin seeds

Dipping sauce
1 spring onion, finely chopped
1 shallot, peeled and finely chopped
20g ginger, finely chopped
dash of oil
1 slice of dried liquorice
180g rock sugar
175g sugar
1 tbsp oyster sauce
130ml light soy sauce
1 tbsp dark soy sauce
2 tbsp Maggi seasoning
a pinch of five-spice powder

Ginger relish
50g ginger
100ml vegetable oil
10g spring onion, finely chopped
5ml sesame oil
sugar, to taste

Soy chicken

Soy sauce chicken is often seen hanging in the windows of restaurants in Hong Kong alongside roast goose and duck. It has a burnished brown skin from its poaching in Chinese master stock, and is glazed with maltose and sesame oil. Andrew recommends visiting a Cantonese roast meat restaurant in person in order to see how chicken is traditionally carved to order.

Poaching liquor Sweat off the ginger in a dash of oil in a large saucepan until fragrant, then add the spring onion and cook for a minute or so before adding the remaining ingredients. Bring to the boil and simmer, stirring occasionally, until all the rock sugar and red yeast rice have dissolved. Set aside.

Dipping sauce Sweat off the spring onion, shallots and ginger in a dash of oil until fragrant. Add the dried liquorice followed by all the remaining ingredients and 250ml water. Bring to the boil and then simmer gently, stirring occasionally, until all the sugar has dissolved and the liquid has reduced to a syrup-like consistency. Set aside to cool.

Ginger relish Peel the ginger and smash it with the side of a cleaver. Finely mince the smashed ginger and transfer to a heatproof bowl or saucepan.

Carefully heat the vegetable oil until it is almost smoking, then pour the hot oil over the minced ginger. Stir together carefully, then add the spring onion. Wait until the relish is cool enough to taste, then add the sesame oil and season with sugar and salt. Set aside to cool completely.

Soy sauce chicken Bring the poaching liquor back to the boil and carefully add the chicken to the pan. Cover with a lid and poach for 50 minutes. After 50 minutes, insert a meat thermometer into the thickest part of the chicken thigh – it should register 74°C.

Remove the chicken from the liquor and allow any excess liquid to drain from the cavity. Hang the chicken using a hook and drain for 10 minutes more. Once drained, brush the maltose all over the chicken then allow to set for 10 minutes before brushing with sesame oil. Rest for 30 minutes.

To serve Cut the chicken into bite sized pieces and serve with the dipping sauce and ginger relish on the side.

Chantelle Nicholson's Mayfair restaurant Apricity is the expression of the forward-thinking ethos which has earned her a reputation as a champion of true sustainability. Its hyper-seasonal menus celebrate locally foraged ingredients, with one tasting menu dedicated to British vegetables and another putting the best meat and fish from across the British Isles centre stage. Whether it's her green approach to sourcing, commitment to wasting nothing or focus on team wellbeing, Chantelle has ensured sustainability is the beating heart of Apricity. It's a devotion which was recognised by Michelin inspectors in 2023, who awarded the restaurant a green star, cementing Chantelle's position as one of the country's most innovative chefs.

Chantelle Nicholson

Left: A focus on team
wellbeing is another core
tenet of Chantelle's ethos
as a chef.

Previous page: Chantelle's
philosophy at Apricity is
centred around the use of
sustainable, seasonal
ingredients and ensuring that
very little goes to waste.

Right: Chantelle puts the
finishing touches to her
rhubarb dessert.

Serves 4
1 hour
Equipment: Stick blender

1 white cabbage, cut into quarters
3 tbsp rose harissa
1 tbsp apple cider vinegar
2 tablespoons rapeseed oil
1 tbsp chopped coriander

Pickled shallots
60g pickle brine (from gherkins, capers or other pickles)
1 banana shallot, peeled and sliced into 2 mm rounds

Miso aioli
50g aquafaba
25g miso
1 tsp Dijon mustard
1 garlic clove, peeled and finely grated
200ml pomace oil
1 tbsp apple cider vinegar

Crispy chickpeas
2 tablespoons rapeseed oil
120g cooked chickpeas (half a 400g tin)
½ tsp ground cumin
1 tbsp cornflour
4 tbsp rapeseed oil

To serve
nasturtium leaves

Harissa-roasted cabbage, miso aioli, pickled shallots, crispy chickpeas

Punchy quarters of cabbage roasted in harissa form the base of this show-stopping vegan recipe from Chantelle, which is a lesson in contrasting flavours and textures. Aquafaba is used in place of egg to make a miso aioli, there's a touch of sharpness from pickled shallots, and crunch from fried chickpeas. Serve this as a starter or part of a sharing spread.

Cabbage Preheat the oven to 200°C.

Remove a few leaves of the cabbage and thinly slice them to make the slaw. Set aside for later.

Mix the harissa paste with an equal amount of water. Brush the outside of the cabbage wedges and in between the leaves with the water and harissa mixture. Season the cabbage with a little salt, then roast for 15-20 minutes, or until nicely browned on the outside and cooked through. If you poke the thickest part of the stem with a skewer there shouldn't be any resistance.

Pickled shallots Place the pickle brine into a small saucepan and gently warm for a few minutes. Remove from the heat and add the sliced shallots. Leave to pickle for 15 minutes.

Miso aioli Place the aquafaba, miso, mustard and garlic into a tall jug. Use a stick blender to blend all the ingredients. Slowly drizzle the oil in, little by little, blending as you go until emulsified. This needs to be done with a stick blender, and won't work if done by hand. Add the vinegar and blend one last time.

Crispy chickpeas Place the chickpeas into a bowl and add the cumin, cornflour and salt to taste. Heat the rapeseed oil in a non-stick frying pan. When hot, add the chickpeas and cook until crispy.

Coleslaw To finish, mix the reserved sliced cabbage with the apple cider vinegar and rapeseed oil. Season with salt and add the coriander. Mix again.

To serve Divide the crispy chickpeas between four plates, then top each one with a wedge of cabbage. Dot the miso aioli around the plate then top with the slaw. Finish with the pickled shallots, and some nasturtium leaves.

Serves 4
1 hour plus chilling and freezing time

200g rhubarb
100g caster sugar
120g cream cheese
50g double cream
1 tsp icing sugar, sieved
2 digestive biscuits, crumbled
Thai basil leaves, to garnish

Poached rhubarb, cheesecake cream, rhubarb granita
In this celebration of rhubarb, Chantelle serves the brightly coloured stalks in a few different ways: poached, raw and diced, and frozen into a granita. A digestive crumb and a sweetened cream cheese complete the recipe to give the impression of a deconstructed cheesecake.

Rhubarb Cut a 10 cm length from a rhubarb stalk, then use a vegetable peeler to peel off 8 thin strips. Dice the remainder of the piece very finely. Set aside the strips and diced rhubarb for later and cut the remaining rhubarb into 3 cm lengths.

Place the caster sugar into a large saucepan. Add 300ml water and bring to the boil. Remove from the heat and add the 3cm lengths of rhubarb. Place on a very low heat for 4 minutes, then check the rhubarb – it should have a very slight give. Once cooked, remove the rhubarb from the pan with a slotted spoon and refrigerate.

Rhubarb granita Reserve 100ml of the liquid then place the rest into a shallow tray and into the freezer to freeze. Once the 100ml has cooled, add the peeled rhubarb strips and transfer to the fridge.

Cheesecake cream Whisk together the cream cheese, cream and icing sugar and refrigerate until needed.

To serve Divide the rhubarb pieces between four plates. Place the digestive crumbs next to the rhubarb, then, using a hot spoon, rocher the cheesecake cream and place on top of the crumb. Loop the peeled strips on top of the poached rhubarb, and garnish with the diced rhubarb.

Scrape up the frozen rhubarb syrup into a granita to spoon over the cheesecake cream. Garnish the dish with basil leaves.

Nokx Majozi

Pie-making is an art form for Nokx Majozi, who creates masterfully intricate pastry designs as head pie-maker at the capital's Holborn Dining Room, taking cues from her South African roots to blend tradition with modernity.

Serves 8
2 hours 30 minutes
Equipment: 20 cm
loose-bottomed cake tin

Cape Malay chicken curry
1kg boneless, skinless chicken thighs
2 tbsp vegetable oil
1 large onion, chopped
20g garlic, minced
20g ginger, minced
5g ground turmeric
3g ground cinnamon
5g ground cumin
400g tin of chopped tomatoes
30g mango or apricot chutney
250ml chicken stock
20g fresh coriander, chopped

Hot water pastry with turmeric
200g plain flour
300g strong flour
10g ground turmeric
4 eggs
150g lard

Cape Malay chicken curry pie

Nokx Majozi's pies are truly the stuff of legend – elegantly decorated and lacquered with an egg yolk glaze, they look and taste divine. This pie is inspired by classic Cape Malay curry: the tangy chicken filling is made with apricot chutney and tomatoes, and the traditional turmeric-infused yellow rice swapped out for amber-hued hot water pastry.

Cape Malay chicken curry Cut the chicken into bite-size pieces and season. Heat the oil in a large pan over medium-high heat and sear the chicken on all sides in batches. Set aside.

Reduce the heat to medium and cook the onion until soft and lightly browned, 6-8 minutes. Add the garlic and ginger and cook for 2 minutes longer, or until fragrant, then stir in the spices.

Add the tomatoes, chutney, stock and chicken. Cover and cook for 15-20 minutes, or until tender, stirring occasionally.

Season with more salt and pepper to taste, then add the coriander. Set aside to cool completely.

Hot water pastry with turmeric Whisk together both flours with the turmeric and 10g salt in the bowl of a stand mixer. Beat together two of the eggs and pass through a fine mesh sieve into the flour. Combine using the paddle attachment.

Bring 150ml water and lard to a boil, then slowly pour into the flour and egg mixture, beating as you go. Scrape the bowl and the paddle halfway through to prevent any lumps. Once well combined, transfer to a lined tray and cover with more baking parchment. Transfer to the fridge to chill.

To assemble Preheat the oven to 200°C.

Roll out the pastry to 1.5 cm thickness, then set aside a third for the lid. Roll out the remaining pastry to line the 20 cm tin.

Grease the base and sides of the tin, then line with the pastry. Trim some of the excess, but leave plenty hanging over the edges. Chill for 5 minutes.

Once chilled, fill with the chicken curry then level the top.

Roll out the remaining third of the pastry until it's large enough to cover the tin. Beat together the remaining two eggs, and generously brush the edge of the pie where it connects to the lid.

Add the lid and press the edge down firmly, ensuring it's tightly sealed. Trim and crimp the edge.

To serve Create a steam hole in the centre of the pie with a knife, and brush the lid with egg wash. Bake on a tray in the oven for 40-50 min or until golden and crisp. Cool in the tin.

At his terracotta-toned Marylebone restaurant KOL, Santiago Lastra is doing something truly unique. By bringing together the flavours and techniques from his home in Mexico with the best British ingredients, he shines a light on Mexican cuisine in a unique way. His approach at KOL has won him acclaim in the form of a Michelin star and a place in the list of the top one hundred restaurants in the world, but even more importantly to him, it has allowed him to show Londoners how special Mexican food can be at its best.

Santiago Lastra

Left: Santiago applies his detail-oriented approach to every single element of his dish, including the pickled shallots served alongside his lamb barbacoa.

Left: KOL's open kitchen is the focal point at the centre of the restaurant, giving diners a glimpse of Santiago and his team at work.

Below: Santiago chooses the leaves for wrapping his lamb barbacoa. The leaves trap steam and keep the lamb succulent during its long, slow cooking time.

Serves 6
5 hours
Equipment: Superbag or muslin,
blender, spray bottle, twine

Nettle sauce
2g kombu
oil, for deep-frying
14g nettles
4g árbol chilli
20g cavolo nero
4ml apple cider vinegar

Barbacoa
1 lamb shoulder, around 2kg
5 ancho chillies
large edible leaves such as spring
greens, banana leaves, leek tops or
kale, for wrapping the lamb

Pickled shallots
3 shallots, peeled but left whole
50ml apple cider vinegar
50ml water
50ml honey

Sesame and chilmole cream
20g chilmole paste
30g sesame seeds
40g Spanish onion, finely chopped
16ml chilmole oil
2g roasted garlic
25g cashews

To serve
5g chicken glace
edible flowers, for garnish
tortillas

Lamb barbacoa

Barbacoa is a rich dish of meat that is rubbed with chillies, wrapped in pointed maguey (agave) leaves and, traditionally, slow-cooked in an underground oven. This dish is an adaptation of the classic, cooked indoors rather than outside, and made using lamb rather than the traditional beef. It's served with a kombu-infused nettle sauce and a sesame and chilmole cream.

Nettle sauce Soak the kombu in 120ml water overnight. The next day, remove and discard the kombu, reserving the water.

Heat 3 cm of oil to 190°C and add the nettles. Cook for 1 minute, or until just toasted. Remove nettles from the oil and drain on paper towels. Blend the nettles with the árbol chilli, cavolo nero, vinegar and seaweed water until smooth, then pass the sauce through a chinois or fine mesh sieve. Season with salt and chill.

Barbacoa Preheat the oven to 140°C.

Deseed the chillies and discard the tough stems. Blend them to a coarse powder in a blender, and rub all over the lamb shoulder. Season the lamb generously with salt. Wrap the lamb shoulder in leaves, using twine to keep them secure.

Prepare a roasting tray full of water and place it in the bottom of the oven. Add the lamb on the rack above and cook for 5 hours, topping up the water as necessary.

Pickled shallots Coat the shallots in a little oil, then cook whole on a plancha or heavy griddle pan until golden, before slicing and seasoning with salt. Combine with the vinegar, water and honey.

Sesame and chilmole cream Blend the chilmole paste and 60ml water together and pass through some muslin.

Toast the sesame seeds in a dry pan until golden.

In a separate pan, cook the onions with the chilmole oil until softened but not coloured. Add the roasted garlic and cook for 30 seconds. Add the chilmole water and mix well, then simmer for 5 minutes.

Blend the sesame seeds to a paste, then add the chilmole and onion mix and blend until smooth. Pass the sauce through a fine mesh strainer.

Toast the cashews in a dry pan until golden brown, then blend with 75g sesame cream until smooth. Season with salt, then transfer to a container and refrigerate.

To serve Pull and chop the lamb shoulder meat into small pieces, around 0.5 cm square. Mix the meat with the chicken glace in a bowl. Decorate the chilmole sauce and pickles with edible flowers.

Serve the sauces, tortillas and pickles on the side.

Serves 12
1 hour 45 minutes, plus freezing time
Equipment: Piping bag,
7 cm round cutter

Dough
56g butter
13g sugar
140g plain flour
1 egg

Chocolate
70g whole milk
160g double cream
1 egg
170g chocolate, chopped
7g mezcal

To serve
vegetable oil, for deep-frying
100g ancho chilli powder
100g brown sugar
20g pork crackling, chopped

Churros

These churro spirals are dusted with a generous mixture of brown sugar and smoky ancho chilli powder, then topped with a disc of mezcal-infused semi-frozen chocolate ganache. Santiago finishes the dish with a sprinkling of crunchy pork crackling, for the ultimate sweet and salty dessert.

Dough Bring 250g water, butter, 2g fine salt and sugar to the boil in a pan. Add the flour and cook out for 5 minutes, making sure it's completely incorporated.

Transfer the dough to a bowl and use an electric whisk or stand mixer to beat the dough at medium speed for 5 minutes. Check the temperature of the dough, and, once it's below 40°C, add the egg and continue mixing for 5 minutes on medium.

Transfer to a piping bag and refrigerate until cool. Once cool, pipe the cold mix into 12 cm diameter flat spirals, about 30g of mixture per spiral. Freeze until solid.

Chocolate While the churros freeze, make the chocolate. Bring the milk and cream to 70°C, then whisk in the egg. Bring the mixture up to 82°C, stirring frequently. Add the chocolate and mezcal and mix well.

Pour the mixture out onto a tray – it should be about 2 mm thick. Use an offset spatula to help spread it out evenly. Allow to set, then cut into discs with the 7 cm cutter.

Transfer the discs to the freezer in a flat layer to set firmly.

To serve Heat a few centimetres of oil to 190°C in a high-sided saucepan. Fry the frozen churros until golden brown, then drain on paper towels.

Mix the ancho chilli powder and brown sugar in a mixing bowl, then transfer to the tray. Add the churros to the chilli sugar, and toss to completely cover.

Transfer the churros to a plate and top each one with a chocolate disc. Use a blow torch to slightly melt the chocolate, then top it with a sprinkling of pork crackling.

In 2013, Tommy Banks took charge of the kitchen at his parents' Yorkshire pub The Black Swan and in doing so became the youngest chef in the UK to hold a Michelin star. In the decade since then, he has only gone from strength to strength, opening the now Michelin-starred Roots in York and becoming a regular on television, all whilst continuing to set the benchmark incredibly high for farm-to-table dining in the UK at The Black Swan. His complex, contemporary dishes are packed full of technique but at their core lies the exceptional produce grown on the family farm.

Tommy Banks

Below: Tommy dresses asparagus with dramatic lines of black garlic emulsion to accompany his beef dish.

Right: Polytunnels at The Black Swan are kept warm using excess heat from the restaurant's generator, and are used to grow ingredients that can't be cultivated outside on Tommy's farm.

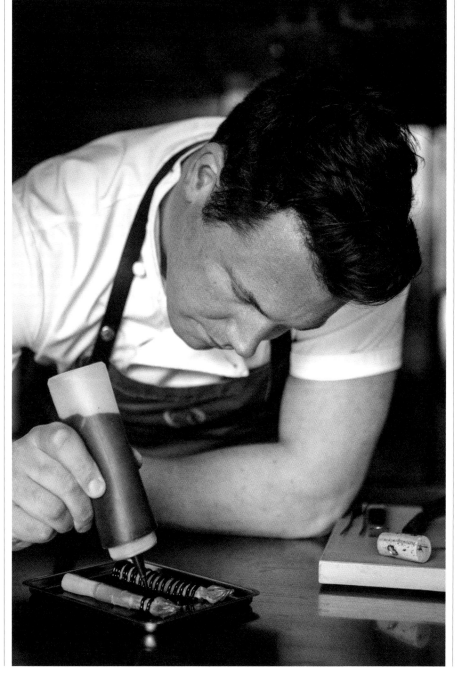

Right: Tommy brushes
truffle butter onto
caramelised scallops.

Serves 6
7 hours, plus infusing time
Equipment: High-powered blender,
muslin cloth

Chive oil
400g chives
400g rapeseed oil

Black garlic emulsion
125g black garlic
190g sunflower oil
50g chicken glace
19g black garlic vinegar
13g Dijon mustard
110g black garlic pulp
110g black garlic oil

Bordelaise sauce
500g chicken wings
500g beef rib bones
butter, for basting
1kg beef trimmings, diced
500g Roscoff onions, sliced
15g thyme
1 star anise
1 large garlic clove
1 bottle of red wine
½ a bottle of ruby port

Chive emulsion
40g egg yolk
15g Dijon mustard
15g caper brine
150-200ml chive oil

Roasted barrel fillet
1kg barrel fillet, trussed for roasting
with extra rendered fat for brushing
oil, for cooking
butter, for cooking

Asparagus
6 asparagus, trimmed
ice water

To serve
rendered beef fat
15g confit shallot,
very finely chopped
25g lardo, finely diced
nasturtium leaves
micro lovage

Barbecued barrel fillet with asparagus

The simple presentation of this stunning beef recipe belies the skill involved. The final result is, however, well worth the effort.

Chive oil Blend chives and oil together in a high-powered blender. Infuse in the fridge for 48 hours, then strain.

Black garlic emulsion Blend the black garlic with the oil until smooth (10 minutes). Infuse overnight, then strain the garlic out using muslin.

Combine the glace, mustard and vinegar and warm to 50°C, then blend. Drizzle the black garlic oil into the blender while running. Add the pulp bit by bit and season. Transfer to a piping bag.

Bordelaise sauce Preheat the oven to 220°C.

Cover wings with water, bring to the boil and cook for 2 hours. Strain the stock and reserve. Transfer the bones to an oven tray.

Roast the bones until golden, then add to the stockpot with the reserved stock. Deglaze the tray with water, then add to the pot.

Add the ribs to the stockpot, bring to a simmer, and cook for 2 hours, topping up with water occasionally as needed.

While the stock is cooking, add a generous amount of butter to a pan, and cook until foaming. Add the beef trimmings and cook until browned, then remove from the pan. Add the onions, thyme and star anise and garlic and cook for 10-15 minutes. Deglaze with water, then add the trimmings and everything in the pan to the stockpot.

Cook the stock for 2 hours, adding water if necessary. Pass through muslin then return the liquid to the pot. Bring to a simmer then reduce by half slowly, skimming frequently.

Add the wine and port to a separate pan and reduce by two thirds, until syrupy. Add the port and wine reduction to the stock.

Chive emulsion Blend together the egg yolk, Dijon mustard and caper brine. Scrape the sides of the blender, then add the chive oil (reserve a little for serving) in a stream with the blender running. If the emulsion is too thick, add a dash of water. If it's too thin, add more oil. Season with salt and transfer to a piping bag.

Roast barrel fillet Preheat the oven to 180°C.

Oil beef and brown on all sides. Baste with butter for 3 minutes.

Transfer to an oven tray, glaze in black garlic emulsion, then roast for 2 minutes. Turn over and glaze again. Cook for another 2 minutes. Repeat until the core temperature reaches 48°C. Rest for 5-8 minutes – we do this in warm clarified butter.

Asparagus Cook the asparagus in salted water for 2-3 minutes. Transfer to ice water.

To serve Warm the sauce with the confit shallot. Carve the beef and brush with beef fat. Split the sauce with some chive oil, beef fat and lardo.

Plate the asparagus and beef. Pipe black garlic emulsion across the asparagus, and chive emulsion in between. Dress with nasturtium and lovage, and spoon the sauce over the beef.

Serves 4-6
2 hours, plus 48 hours for the glaze
to ferment
Equipment: 1.5 cm teardrop shaped
cutter, muslin

Celeriac and sourdough glaze
200g medium slices of sourdough
1g fresh yeast
2g caster sugar
Chardonnay vinegar, to taste

Celeriac pickle
100ml white wine vinegar
100g sugar
100g celeriac, cut into 2 mm
thick slices

Celeriac velouté
85g unsalted butter
1kg celeriac, very thinly sliced
(save the peelings)
750ml white chicken stock
150ml double cream
Chardonnay vinegar

Celeriac powder
celeriac peelings, washed

Truffle butter
125g unsalted butter
50g frozen truffle

Celeriac salad
25g celery, finely diced
5g celery leaves, thinly sliced
25g celeriac, finely diced
15g frozen truffle, finely diced
15g hazelnut, finely diced
hazelnut oil, to taste

Scallop
4-6 XXL hand-dived king scallops
2 tbsp oil
50g butter

To serve
celeriac powder

Scallop, celeriac and truffle

Use the biggest king scallops you can get hold of for this indulgent recipe. Tommy bastes them in a luxurious truffle butter and transforms celeriac in several ways, including a velvety velouté.

Celeriac and sourdough glaze Preheat the oven to 180°C and place the bread on oven trays in a single layer.

Toast until dark golden and crisp – 10-20 minutes. Cool.

Break the bread into pieces and transfer to a container. Top them with 800ml water, then weigh down to keep the bread submerged. Infuse for 24 hours at room temperature.

Transfer the bread to some muslin, and squeeze out as much water as possible. Discard the solids, then add the yeast and sugar to the liquid. Ferment for 24 hours at room temperature.

Add chardonnay vinegar to taste, then reduce the liquid to a glaze-like consistency. Refrigerate until needed.

Celeriac pickle Bring all ingredients except the celeriac to the boil with 100ml water over medium heat. Set aside to cool. Cut out the slices of celeriac with the teardrop-shaped cutter.

Pour the brine over the celeriac and refrigerate for 24 hours.

Celeriac velouté Melt the butter and add the celeriac and a pinch of salt. Cook over a low heat for 10-15 minutes until softened but not coloured. Add the stock and bring to a boil. Add the cream and bring to a simmer, then remove from the heat.

Blend the celeriac velouté until smooth, then season to taste with salt and chardonnay vinegar.

Celeriac powder Roast the washed skins at 160°C until browned, but not burnt. Leave to cool and dry overnight, then blend to a powder.

Truffle butter Melt the butter in a small saucepan over medium heat. Turn the heat up slightly, and continue to cook until the milk solids turn brown and the butter smells nutty, stirring frequently. Take care that the milk solids at the bottom don't burn.

Pour off the clarified butter, leaving the browned milk solids in the pan. Blend the clarified brown butter with the frozen truffle, and chill until needed.

Celeriac salad Mix everything together, adding salt and hazelnut oil to taste.

To serve Warm the celeriac velouté with 1 tablespoon of the truffle butter.

Heat a heavy pan over high heat with a dash of oil. Dress the scallops with oil and a generous amount of salt.

Add the scallops to the pan and cook until deeply caramelised. Turn them over and add the butter. Once the butter begins to foam, baste the scallops until fully cooked.

Remove from the pan and brush with the glaze.

Add a spoonful of the salad to the centre of each bowl. Spoon the velouté around and place a scallop in the centre. Top each with some celeriac pickle, and then dust it with celeriac powder.

Helen Graham

You won't find any meat on executive chef Helen Graham's menu at Middle Eastern concept Bubala in London. Instead, the former-Ottolenghi chef is winning plaudits for demonstrating how vegetables can play a starring role in every dish when treated with enough care and attention.

Serves 6
2 hours, plus time for the labneh to strain overnight
Equipment: Muslin

Preserved lemon labneh
500g Greek yoghurt
1 preserved lemon, finely chopped

Saffron-braised fennel
2 fennel bulbs
125g unsalted butter, diced
100g sugar
1 tbsp moscatel or red wine vinegar
pinch oM saffron
2 tbsp vegetable oil

Black olive salsa
100g black olives, de-stoned and finely chopped
1 garlic clove, finely grated
1 tbsp maple syrup
1 tbsp Moscatel or red wine vinegar
zest of ½ an orange (optional)
1½ tbsp soy sauce
¼ tsp black pepper
1 bunch of parsley, finely chopped
100ml olive oil

Saffron-braised fennel, preserved lemon labneh and black olive salsa

This saffron-infused dish from Helen Graham is a delicious way to serve fennel, as slow-braising mellows fennel's aniseed flavour, rendering it sweet and tender. The labneh is made from scratch by hanging salted Greek yoghurt overnight, but you could use shop-bought labneh.

Preserved lemon labneh Transfer the yoghurt to a mixing bowl and whisk in ½ a teaspoon table salt. Set a colander lined with a j-cloth or piece of muslin above a bowl and transfer the yoghurt to the colander. Cover the yoghurt with another j-cloth or piece of muslin, and transfer to the fridge to drain overnight.

The next day, transfer the labneh back into a bowl and beat in the preserved lemon. Set aside until ready to serve.

Saffron braised fennel Preheat the oven to 180°C.

Melt the butter with the sugar, ½ a teaspoon table salt, 500ml water, vinegar and saffron on a medium heat. Whisk the mixture until the sugar and salt have dissolved.

Cut each fennel into quarters lengthways. Place the fennel cut-side-up in a deep oven tray. Pour the butter mixture over the fennel and cover the tray with foil. Transfer the fennel to the oven and cook for 45 minutes, turning halfway through.

Remove the fennel from the liquid and set aside to cool. Reserve the liquid for serving.

Black olive salsa Place the olives, garlic, maple syrup, vinegar, orange zest, soy sauce, black pepper and parsley in a bowl and mix together. Slowly whisk in the olive oil, then set aside.

To serve Heat the vegetable oil over medium-high heat in a frying pan, and then add the fennel. Sear the fennel for a couple minutes on each side, or until golden.

Turn the heat up to high and add a few spoonfuls of the braising liquid. Cook until the braising liquid has been reduced by half – it should form a thick syrup that would coat the back of a spoon. Taste the syrup for seasoning, and adjust as needed.

Smooth the labneh onto a serving platter, then place the glazed fennel pieces on top. Pour the remaining reduced saffron caramel over the fennel. Spoon over the black olive salsa and serve.

Shuko Oda first launched Soho's Koya over a decade ago, her freshly-made, traditional udon noodles and dashi quickly garnering praise. Since then, Koya has become a cherished London institution, growing to three sites across the capital. Having spent much of her life living between London, Tokyo and Los Angeles, Shuko deftly blends authentic Japanese cooking with seasonal British produce. Those ingredients play a starring role in Koya's food, including its specials: modern Japanese dishes which go beyond the more familiar options. Shuko's cooking has not only earned her a reputation as one of the capital's most vibrant chefs, but it's also broadened our understanding of Japanese cuisine.

Shuko Oda

Left: Shuko's striking dish of winter tomatoes, nori and home-made fermented tofu.

Left: Shuko plates up in the kitchen at Koya City, the second of her three restaurants.

Below: Wisps of monk's beard (agretti) add a final flourish to a colourful bowl of chirashi zushi.

Serves 4, a starter
1 hour 30 minutes, plus 3 weeks
for the tofu to ferment
Equipment: Blender

550g winter tomatoes
ice water, as needed

Fermented Tofu
200g firm tofu
50ml sake

Tofu sauce
100g fermented tofu
1 tbsp roasted sesame seeds
½ tsp roasted sesame oil
½ tbsp sugar
½ tbsp mirin
4g miso

Nori sauce
10g nori, torn into small pieces
½ tbsp soy sauce
1 tbsp mirin
1 tbsp sake

Garnish
12 nasturtium leaves

Winter tomatoes, nori and fermented tofu

Chilled tomato salads are a popular side dish in Japan, perfect for combatting the oppressive heat and humidity of summer. Here Shuko Oda adds a creamy fermented tofu dressing and a simple nori sauce to this elegant side dish.

Fermented Tofu Wrap some paper towels or a clean tea towel around the tofu, and place a plate on top. Top the plate with a heavy frying pan or chopping board, and let the tofu press for at least 30 minutes – this will remove some of the liquid from the tofu.

To make the brine, mix together the sake, 60g fine sea salt and 500ml water. Whisk to make sure that all the salt is dissolved. The brine needs to be 12% salt and 10% sake.

Add the pressed tofu, making sure it is completely submerged in the brine. You can cut it into smaller cubes if it's too big. Cover with an airtight lid and leave to ferment at room temperature for 3 weeks, then store in the fridge.

Tofu sauce Grind the sesame seeds in a pestle and mortar until finely ground and paste-like.

Heat the mirin and sugar in a saucepan to dissolve the sugar and cook off the alcohol in the mirin. Add the mixture to a blender with the sesame, 100g of fermented tofu, sesame oil, miso and 1 tablespoon water. Blend until the paste is smooth and glossy.

Nori sauce Simmer all the ingredients in a pan with 100ml water for 5 minutes, stirring occasionally.

Tomatoes Bring a large pan of water to the boil. Score the bottom of each tomato with a cross and place in the water until the skin starts to peel and pull back. Transfer the tomatoes to a bowl of ice water, then peel the skin off the tomatoes. Cut them into even quarters.

To serve Press the tomato quarters back together so that the tomato looks whole again and place one 'whole' tomato in each bowl.

Gently spoon some tofu sauce on top, then add the nori sauce. Garnish with nasturtium leaves.

Serves 4
2 hours 30 minutes,
plus overnight pickling
Equipment: Mandoline

Beetroot pickle
200g golden beetroot
65ml rice vinegar
18g sugar
5 cm piece of kombu
½ dried red chilli, deseeded

Herring
5 herrings, roughly 80g each
54g sugar
108g soy sauce
36g mirin
36g sake
10g ginger, washed and sliced
1 tsp dried Sichuan peppercorns

Rice
300g rice
45g rice vinegar
20g sugar

To serve
30g monk's beard
2 tbsp roasted sesame seeds
edible flowers, as needed
ice water, as needed

Chirashi zushi with candied herring, golden beetroot and monk's beard

Chirashi zushi – or scattered sushi – is a great introduction to making sushi at home as it doesn't require any rolling or shaping of the rice. Instead, seasoned rice is simply 'scattered' with different colourful toppings. Here, Shuko Oda combines British ingredients such as herring, beetroot and monk's beard with Japanese techniques.

Beetroot pickle Peel and slice the golden beetroot on a mandoline to 1-2 mm thick discs. Bring the rice, vinegar and sugar for the pickle to a boil with 8g salt and 160ml water, stirring to dissolve. Set aside to cool.

Once cool, add the kombu, chilli and beetroot to the brine and transfer to the fridge to pickle for 24 hours.

Herring The next day, prepare the herring. Clean the fish thoroughly, taking care to wash off any remaining blood and guts. Pat the fish dry.

Place the herrings in a small pan so that they fit snugly. Add the remaining herring ingredients and 300ml water and bring to the boil. Lower the heat to a simmer, then place a sheet of foil directly on top of the herring. Scrunch up the edges of the foil to make a circular shape, then cut a small hole in the middle for steam to escape. This allows the herring to keep their shape, cook evenly and for the sauce to penetrate the whole fillet.

Simmer the fish for 1 hour 30 minutes, or until the liquid is reduced by half, thickened and coats the fish. Set aside to cool, then gently debone the fillets.

Rice Place the rice in a bowl and cover with water. Gently mix the rice, then pour away the starchy water. Repeat five times, then soak the rice in 2 litres of water for 1 hour.

Drain the soaked rice, then allow it to dry for 30 minutes. Add the drained rice to a pot with 430ml water and top with a lid. Bring to a boil over a medium heat, then turn the heat down to low and cook for 10 minutes. Turn the heat off, leave the lid on and let the rice steam for 10 minutes. While the rice steams, mix together the vinegar, sugar and 6g salt to make the sushi vinegar.

Take the lid off and gently mix the rice, drizzling over the sushi vinegar. Transfer to a large serving plate and spread out to a 3 cm thick layer. Fan the rice with a magazine or newspaper to cool it down – you want it to be roughly body temperature.

To serve Bring a small pan of water to the boil. Chop the roots off the monk's beard, then add to the water. Cook for 20 seconds, then use tongs to transfer to a bowl of ice water. Drain and cut into 5 cm lengths.

Quarter the pieces of beetroot. Spread the pickles over the rice with care, then add the herring and a few spoonfuls of brine and some peppercorns. Sprinkle over the sesame seeds, then add the monk's beard and edible flowers.

Few chefs have made their mark on Britain's restaurant scene more than Simon Rogan. A true master of his art, Simon first opened his flagship restaurant L'Enclume in the Cumbrian village of Cartmel in 2002 and over time it is has gradually evolved into one of the best restaurants in the country, if not the world. With a philosophy centred around using only the best ingredients, which have mostly either been foraged locally or supplied by his own farm in the Cartmel Valley, to create highly complex dishes, he has long been one of the chefs at the core of the 'seasonal British' movement. It was no surprise therefore, when Simon won the rare accolade of three Michelin stars in 2022.

Simon Rogan

Above: Simon garnished his
dish of Musselburgh leeks
with a variety of sorrels,
all grown on site.

Below: At Our Farm, everything from vegetables and herbs to edible flowers are grown in polytunnels, giving Simon and his team immediate access to exceptional seasonal produce.

Serves 4
4 hours, plus time for the quinoa
vinegar to infuse overnight
Equipment: Piping bag, muslin

Quinoa vinegar gel
50g black quinoa
250ml white wine vinegar
30g sugar
2g agar

Puffed quinoa
oil, for deep-frying

Confit egg yolks
oil, for cooking
500g chicken wings,
cut into 2-3 cm pieces
500g butter
4 copper Marans egg yolks

Miso butter
75g red miso
75g butter
50g cream
25g shallot
50g mead
50g crème fraîche

Confit leek
280g leeks (trimmed weight)
5 fennel seeds
2 white peppercorns
ice water

To serve
mixed oxalis, such as burgundy
oxalis, sunset oxalis and
oxalis flowers

Musselburgh leeks, quinoa and assorted sorrels, Marans egg yolk cooked in chicken fat

This show-stopping leek recipe requires a bit of patience but is well worth the effort. Simon uses biodynamic Musselburgh leeks, cooked in miso butter – at L'Enclume the miso is made from quinoa and red beans but shop-bought miso works equally well. Likewise, puffed quinoa can be bought to save time.

Quinoa vinegar gel Toast the quinoa in a dry pan for a few minutes, then add to the vinegar. Infuse for 24 hours.

The next day, strain out the quinoa. Dry it very thoroughly on paper towels and set aside.

Add 70g quinoa vinegar to a pan with 70g water, sugar and agar. If using agar flakes, soak in the liquid for 30 minutes. If using powder, whisk in straight away. Bring to a simmer and cook until the agar has dissolved, about 5 minutes.

Transfer to the fridge. Once set, blend and pass through a fine sieve, then transfer to a piping bag.

Puffed quinoa Preheat the oven to 70°C. Add the pickled quinoa to a lined oven tray, and dry thoroughly in the oven.

Heat a few centimetres of oil to 200°C in a high-sided saucepan. Fry the pickled quinoa in the oil, using a small, heat proof wire mesh strainer to contain it. Season with salt and set aside.

Confit egg yolks Heat a dash of oil in a pan and add the chicken wings. Cook the wings until browned all over, then add the butter. Cook over a low heat for 1 hour then remove from the heat. Let the wings infuse in the butter for an hour, then strain the butter through some muslin, and transfer to a small oven proof dish.

Preheat the oven to 64°C.

Add the egg yolks, ensuring they're completely submerged in the butter. Cook in the oven until the yolks are fudgy, about 1 hour. Check the oven's temperature with a thermometer if possible, and keep checking on the egg yolks every 10 minutes or so.

Miso butter Combine the miso, butter and cream. Chill thoroughly.

Add the shallot and mead to a pan, and cook until the mead has reduced by a quarter. Pass the sauce through a fine sieve.

Add the reduction to a pan with the crème fraîche. Bring to a simmer, then add the miso butter in small pieces, whisking thoroughly after each one. Pass the sauce, adding more cream or butter if necessary to adjust the flavour and texture. Set aside.

Confit leek Wash the leeks very well in running water. Cook in a covered pan with a splash of water and the remaining ingredients plus 15g salt until tender, 5-10 minutes. Chill in ice water.

To serve Slice the leeks into 1 cm cylinders, and gently warm in a pan. Place 50g leeks in the centre of each bowl. Make a well in the centre of the leeks and add the egg yolk. Sprinkle fried quinoa on top, then pipe on six dots of quinoa vinegar gel.

Arrange the mixed oxalis over the leeks. Gently heat 200g of the miso sauce in a pan and pour next to the leeks just before serving.

Serves 4-6
2 hours 30 minutes, plus overnight
infusing and chilling time
Equipment: 3 cm round cutter,
15 × 20 cm loaf tin, piping bag,
ice cream maker

Crème pâtissière
500ml milk
25g sweet cicely
5g chervil
2g lovage
2g mint
0.5g star anise
¼ vanilla pod
108g double cream,
100g lightly whipped
22g sugar
22g egg yolks
5g corn flour
2.5g custard powder

Milk ice cream
1 litre whole milk
100ml double cream
50g milk powder
75g glucose
240g sugar
125g egg yolks

Malwina strawberries
600g strawberries, 500g roughly
chopped, 100g quartered
100g sugar

**Chamomile and
bee pollen milk cake**
150g unsalted butter, room
temperature
150g caster sugar
75g condensed milk
75g eggs
7.5g baking powder
150g T55 flour
2.5g camomile powder
10g bee pollen

Sweet cicely gin
ice water
50g sweet cicely
150g sugar
gin, to taste

To serve
assorted edible leaves and flowers

Malwina strawberries, cream infused with sweet herbs, camomile cake and strawberry juice

This is an elevated take on the age-old combination of strawberries and cream. Late-season Malwina strawberries are macerated and served with a herb-infused crème pâtissière, an unusual milk cake flavoured with chamomile, and milk ice cream.

Crème pâtissière Bring the milk to the boil, remove from the heat and add the herbs, star anise and vanilla. Refrigerate overnight, then strain.

Whisk the sugar, cornflour, custard powder and egg yolks until pale. Bring 8g unwhipped cream and 100g infused milk to a boil, then pour over the egg yolk mixture while whisking constantly.

Transfer the mixture back to the saucepan and cook over a low heat, whisking constantly until it thickens. Set aside to cool.

Once cool, whip together the crème pâtissière with the remaining 100g lightly whipped cream, and transfer to a piping bag.

Milk ice cream Bring the double cream, milk, milk powder and glucose to a simmer, stirring to dissolve. Whisk together the sugar and yolks.

Pour the cream mixture over the yolks in a stream, whisking constantly. Transfer back into the pan and cook to 80°C. Pass through a fine mesh sieve and chill thoroughly, ideally overnight.

Once chilled, churn in an ice cream maker and transfer to the freezer to firm up.

Malwina strawberries Combine the roughly chopped strawberries with the sugar and mix. Macerate overnight.

Strain the juice that has been released through a cheesecloth. Add the quartered strawberries to a container and submerge in the juice. Set aside, reserving any extra strawberry juice.

Chamomile and bee pollen milk cake Preheat the oven to 150°C. Grease and line the tin.

Beat together the butter and sugar then add the condensed milk and mix. Add the egg in two batches, whisking each time.

Sift in the baking powder and flour. Mix, then add the camomile and pollen. Mix, pour into the tin and bake for ~40 minutes.

Once cooked, cool in the tin for 10 minutes. Transfer to a rack. Once cold, trim the edges and cut into discs.

Sweet cicely gin Bring a pot of water to the boil and add the sweet cicely. Blanch for a few seconds then transfer to the ice water.

Make a syrup by combining 200g water and sugar in a pan. Cook, stirring occasionally, until all the sugar has dissolved.

Blitz the syrup with the sweet cicely, then add gin to taste.

To serve Cut a 3 cm round out of each cake, brushing with sweet cicely syrup. Add 20g strawberries to each plate, then top with the cake. Pipe some crème pâtissière on top, then make a divot in the cream. Add a quenelle of ice cream. Drizzle over 15g strawberry juice and garnish with edible leaves and flowers.

Richard Bainbridge

Richard Bainbridge puts his training in classical, Michelin-starred cooking to good use at the helm of his hometown restaurant Benedicts in Norwich, where Norfolk produce takes centre stage and creativity shines through in modern, playful menus.

Serves 4
3 hours 30 minutes
Equipment: Pasta machine,
8 cm round cutter, food processor

Herb pasta
1 egg
3 egg yolks
20g soft herbs, such as parsley or coriander
250g 00 pasta flour
dash of Norfolk rapeseed oil

Shellfish bisque
1-2 kg shellfish shells, e.g. prawn, crab or lobster shells, broken up into large pieces
200g brandy
oil, for cooking
4 shallots, peeled and roughly chopped
4 carrots, peeled and roughly chopped
3 sticks of celery, roughly chopped
1 leek, roughly chopped
6 tomatoes, roughly chopped
handful of flat leaf parsley
handful of chervil
handful of tarragon
300g double cream
200g white port
a few drops of lemon juice
50g salted butter

Crab filling
2 dressed Cromer crabs
1 lime, zested and juiced
20g coriander, finely chopped
white pepper

Sauce vierge
4 tomatoes, peeled, deseeded and diced
100ml olive oil
½ lemon, juiced
1 tbsp fresh basil, finely chopped
1⁄2 tbsp chervil, finely chopped
½ garlic clove, finely chopped
3 coriander seeds, crushed

To serve
1 Granny Smith apple, peeled and finely diced
sprigs of chervil

Crab raviolo, shellfish bisque, sauce vierge

This light, elegant starter is perfect for summer when tomatoes are at their best, and makes the most of fresh Cromer crab.

Herb pasta Blend the eggs, yolks and herbs until smooth.

Add the flour and 10g salt to a food processor and pulse to combine. On low, slowly add the egg mixture until it resembles fine breadcrumbs. Add a few drops of rapeseed oil.

Knead until it comes together. Wrap and refrigerate overnight.

Shellfish bisque Preheat the oven to 175°C.

Place the broken shells into a deep tray and roast for 25 minutes.

Remove from the oven and place over a low heat. Add the brandy and white port and flambe. Gently pour into a large saucepan.

Heat a dash of oil in a large frying pan. Cook the shallots until browned. Add the carrots and celery until softened. Add the leek, tomatoes, herbs, 4 litres water and bring to the boil. Turn down to a simmer and cook for 2 hours, skimming occasionally.

Strain the stock into a pot. Bring to the boil and reduce by 3/4. Add the cream and a splash of white port. Season with salt, pepper and a few drops of lemon juice.

Crab filling Remove the white meat from the dressed crabs and place onto a cold tray. Pick through the crab for shell.

Blend the brown meat to a purée. Add 2 tablespoons of the brown meat to the white meat, then add the lime zest, juice and season. Add the coriander refrigerate.

Sauce vierge Combine the tomatoes with the olive oil, lemon juice, herbs, garlic and coriander seeds. Mix gently and season.

Filling the ravioli On a floured surface, roll out the rested dough to 3 mm thickness. Cut rounds using an 8 cm round cutter.

Place a tablespoon of the crab filling in the middle of each disc. Place a disc on top and press the edges together firmly. Moisten the edges with water if needed. Place on a floured surface and cover with a tea towel.

To serve Simmer the ravioli in boiling salted water for 3 minutes. Lightly dry on kitchen towel before serving.

Warm the sauce vierge slightly. Whisk the butter into the shellfish bisque.

Spoon a little sauce vierge into the middle of a bowl and add a cooked raviolo on top. Garnish with few diced apples and chervil. Serve the bisque in a jug.

At his eponymous restaurant tucked away in St James' Market, Ramael Scully has been wowing diners with his vibrant cookery since 2018. His creative, flavour-led dishes take cues from everything from his Malaysian roots to his time spent working with Yotam Ottolenghi whilst also showcasing a flare for presentation. In his kitchen, nothing goes to waste, with the likes of peels and by-products making their way downstairs to his basement kitchen-cum-fermentation lab, where they're transformed into flavour bombs for future menus – a cyclical and effortlessly sustainable approach to fine dining. This has rightfully earned Scully a reputation as one of the capital's most inventive chefs.

Ramael Scully

Below: Scully's pastry chef Adrian Petrovan sprinkles desiccated coconut on top of the chocolate-glazed matcha Swiss roll.

Right: Scully portions his roasted pork belly at the pass of his eponymous restaurant.

Serves 4-6
4 hours 30 minutes
Equipment: 32 cm × 24 cm
baking tray

Roasted pork belly
20 sprigs of thyme
12 large garlic cloves, unpeeled and
lightly crushed with a knife
4 stalks of lemongrass, lightly
bruised with a rolling pin
100g ginger, unpeeled and cut
into 1 cm slices
1.5kg bone-in skin-on pork belly
1 lemon, halved
500ml dry white wine

Cubeb pepper caramel
2 tsp sunflower oil
60g unsalted butter
3 garlic cloves, finely chopped
2 small banana shallots, finely
chopped
2 long red chillies, de-seeded and
finely chopped
2 sprigs fresh curry leaves, leaves
picked
30g dried shrimp, rinsed, patted dry,
then ground with a spice grinder or
pestle and mortar
1½ tbsp caster sugar
1½ tbsp white miso paste
3 tbsp light soy sauce
2 tbsp dark soy sauce
150ml chicken stock
1 tbsp cubeb peppercorns, ground
with a spice grinder or pestle and
mortar until finely ground

Pomelo salsa
¼ pomelo or pink grapefruit, skin
removed and kernels separated
1 small cucumber, deseeded and
finely diced
½ large bulb of fennel, finely diced
1 large celery stalk, finely diced
½ red chilli, deseeded and
finely diced
¼ bunch mint, leaves picked and
finely chopped
¼ bunch coriander, leaves picked
and finely chopped
1 lime, juiced
1 tbsp rapeseed oil

Roasted pork belly, cubeb pepper caramel, pomelo salsa

Scully takes influence from his Malaysian roots for this recipe.
A rich caramel infused with cubeb peppercorns, which are native
to Southeast Asia, sits alongside crispy belly and zingy pomelo
salsa. The caramel can be made in advance and kept in the fridge
for up to a week.

Roasted pork belly Preheat the oven to 240°C.

Add the thyme, garlic, lemongrass and ginger to a roasting tray.
Pat the belly dry, then place on top of the herbs, skin side up. Rub
the skin with cut lemon, squeezing the juice out as you rub. Let sit
for 10 minutes, then sprinkle 30g flaky sea salt evenly over the
skin.

Roast the pork for 1 hour, or until the crackling is semi-crisp and
the salt has turned grey. Don't worry if the aromatics burn before
the pork is done.

Remove the pork from the oven. Scrape off and discard the salt
on the skin. Spread another 30g salt all over the pork skin and
return to the oven. Cook for another 30 minutes, or until the
crackling is completely crisp.

Remove the pork from the oven and turn the heat down to
190°C. Pour 400ml water and the wine into the oven tray,
taking care to avoid the crispy skin and sides of the pork belly.
Use a knife to release air from any bubbles on the skin.

Cook the pork for another hour, then turn the heat down to
120°C and cook for one more hour.

Remove the pork from the oven and rest for at least 30 minutes.

Cubeb pepper caramel Heat the butter and oil until it starts
to foam. Add the garlic and shallots and cook until soft and
translucent, 6-7 minutes. Add the chilli, curry leaves and ground
dried shrimp and cook for 2-3 minutes or until fragrant. Add the
sugar and cook, stirring constantly, until the sugar has
caramelised, about 1 minute more.

Add the miso and stir, then add both soy sauces, the stock and
75ml water. Bring to a simmer and cook for 6 minutes then
remove from the heat and stir in the pepper. Set aside to cool
and infuse. Once cool, it can be blended or served as is.

Pomelo salsa Mix all the ingredients for the salsa together with
some flaky sea salt, and set aside in the fridge.

To serve Brush any excess salt from the skin of the pork.
Use a serrated knife to slice the meat into 3-4 cm thick pieces,
cutting between the ribs.

Add a few spoonfuls of the pomelo salsa to each plate.
Warm up the caramel if necessary, and divide between the
plates. Top with a slice of pork.

Serves 6
3 hours, plus cooling and chilling time
Equipment: Baking tray, electric whisk, blender, piping bag with star tip (optional)

Yoghurt shards
4 egg whites
300g icing sugar
½ tsp cream of tartar
25g yoghurt powder

Lime mascarpone
1½ limes, zested and juiced
50g caster sugar
2 eggs
55g cold butter, cut into small cubes
50g mascarpone
Black sesame ganache
150g white chocolate
30g butter
24g glucose
60g double cream, cold
70g black tahini

Chocolate glaze
125g butter
125g 70% cacao chocolate chips
50g icing sugar
100g desiccated coconut

Pandan syrup
30g pandan leaves, crushed with your hands
100g glucose
100g sugar

Swiss roll
4 eggs, separated
70g icing sugar
8g matcha powder
25g milk, warm
55g rapeseed oil
1 tsp vanilla essence
60g plain flour
½ tsp baking powder
¼ tsp cream of tartar

Raspberry coulis
300g raspberries, fresh or frozen
50g caster sugar
1 tbsp lemon juice

To serve
150g fresh raspberries

Matcha Swiss roll, black tahini ganache, lime mascarpone, yoghurt shards

Ramael Scully takes the traditional Swiss roll and turns it on its head in this playful recipe, swapping traditional berries and cream elements for fun, playful twists.

Yoghurt shards Preheat the oven to 90°C and line a baking tray.

Beat the egg whites until slightly firmer than soft peaks. Fold in the icing sugar, cream of tartar and yoghurt powder. Spread the egg whites onto the tray in a very thin layer. Cook for 2 hours.

Allow the yoghurt cool completely before breaking into shards.

Lime mascarpone Whisk together the lime zest, lime juice, sugar and eggs in a small pan. Place over low heat and whisk constantly until thickened. Add the cold butter cubes one by one, whisking after each addition. If the mixture is loose, transfer to a heatproof bowl and cook over simmering water until it thickens.

Transfer the curd to the fridge. Once cool, fold in the mascarpone. Transfer to a piping bag with a star tip (optional).

Black sesame ganache Melt the white chocolate and butter in a bain-marie. Set aside.

Heat the glucose in a small saucepan until bubbling, then set aside. Fold in the melted white chocolate. It will look grainy, but don't worry. Fold in the double cream and black tahini.

Blend the warm tahini mixture in a blender, then chill.

Chocolate glaze Melt the chocolate chips and butter in a bain-marie. Remove from the heat and whisk in the icing sugar until smooth. Set aside to cool.

Pandan syrup Bring all ingredients and 500ml water to the boil and stir until the sugar is dissolved. Reduce to a low simmer. Cook 10-15 minutes until it forms a light syrup. Set aside to cool.

Swiss roll Preheat the oven to 160°C. Line the baking pan and spray with non-stick cooking spray.

Whisk the yolks and sugar until thick and creamy. Add the matcha, milk, oil and vanilla and whisk again. Sift in the flour and baking powder, cream of tartar and ¼ teaspoon flaky sea salt, then fold in.

Whisk the egg whites to soft peaks, then fold into the yolk mix.

Add the batter to the cake tin in an even layer. Bake for 20 minutes or until it springs back to the touch.

Turn out the slightly cooled cake onto a clean tea towel. Remove the baking parchment, then brush with pandan syrup. Cool completely. Remove the black sesame ganache from the fridge.

Spread a layer of ganache over the cake. Use the tea towel to roll it up. Place on a wire rack over a tray. Pour over the chocolate glaze, then sprinkle with desiccated coconut. Refrigerate.

Raspberry coulis Simmer the ingredients for 10-15 minutes until the raspberries have broken down. Chill.

To serve Slice the roll into pieces. Serve with yoghurt shards, mascarpone and raspberries folded into the coulis.

At the start of summer each year, Amy Elles and her husband Jack reopen their restaurant The Harbour Café, a wooden seafood shack on the Fife coast containing just a few tables. From the tiny kitchen, Amy then serves a stunning seafood-focused menu, which makes use of the bounty of wonderful ingredients found nearby and demonstrates her immense skill at drawing huge flavour out of deceptively simple dishes. This talent is the result of years of experience working in top kitchens including The Fat Duck, as well as running her own catering company, and has rightfully led to Amy's reputation stretching far beyond the bounds of Fife.

Amy Elles

Left: Amy plates up her scallop tartare, surrounding the shell with seaweed foraged from around the restaurant.

Above: At The Harbour Cafe, Amy makes use of the vast array of world-class seafood caught off Scotland's coast.

Serves 4
1 hour, plus time overnight
curing time
Equipment: Clean tea towel

Scallops
4 scallops, in their shell
1 lime, juiced, plus extra for serving

Tomato consommé
3 tomatoes, roughly chopped

Cured fennel
1 fennel bulb, diced
¼ teaspoon fennel seeds, toasted
50g caster sugar
50g white wine vinegar

To serve
¼ cucumber, finely diced
edible flowers and leaves, such as
bronze fennel or sprigs of dill

Cured fennel scallop tartare

Serving scallops in their raw form is one of the best ways to showcase their incredible natural sweetness. Here, Amy Elles dices scallop and combines it with cucumber and cured fennel to make a tartare, which is presented in the shells alongside a tomato consommé for an elegant but fantastically fresh starter.

Cured fennel Mix all the ingredients for the cured fennel except for the fennel with some salt and 50g water. Whisk until the salt and sugar have dissolved. Add the diced fennel and leave to cure overnight.

Tomato consommé Blend the tomatoes with a pinch of salt. Line a bowl with a clean, dry tea towel and add the tomato mixture to the centre. Gather up and tie the ends of the towel so that the tomato pulp is sealed inside.

Either hang the tomato pulp over the bowl and let it drip out naturally overnight or squeeze it by hand to produce a clear tomato consommé. Allowing the liquid to drip out overnight will produce the clearest liquid, but gently squeezing the tomato liquid out will work as well.

Scallops Once the fennel is cured, remove the scallops from the shell. Clean the shells very thoroughly, as these will be used to serve the scallop tartare. Remove the scallop roe and set aside for another dish, then clean the scallop thoroughly.

Dice the scallop meat and mix with the lime juice and a pinch of salt. Gently mix to combine and let cure in the fridge for 10-20 minutes, depending on your taste and the size of the dice.

To serve Spoon a little scallop tartare, cured fennel and cucumber in each scallop shell. Squeeze over some extra lime juice and pour in the tomato consommé. Eat straight away.

Serves 4
1 hour 30 minutes
Equipment: Blender

Rouille
1 medium potato, peeled and
roughly chopped
a pinch of saffron
a pinch of smoked paprika,
or to taste
60g hazelnuts, toasted
5 garlic cloves, roughly chopped
enough fish stock to cover the
potatoes
1 red pepper, roasted and peeled
200ml olive oil
½ lemon

Fish soup
35g unsalted butter
a dash of olive oil
2 celery sticks, sliced
4 carrots, sliced
1 onion, peeled and diced
2 garlic cloves, roughly chopped
5 tomatoes, diced
½ a courgette, sliced
a pinch of smoked paprika
1 inch piece of Noros pepper
a pinch of saffron
3 medium waxy potatoes, peeled
and roughly chopped
enough fish stock to cover
600g smoked haddock, cut into
chunks
600g fresh haddock, cut into chunks
1-2g langoustines per person,
shell on
400g squid tentacles
500g surf clams, soaked in
water for 2 hours to clean,
water changed halfway
300g mussels, cleaned and
debearded

To serve
lemon wedges

Fish soup

Accompanied by a classic rouille, Amy's showstopping fish soup makes the most of Scotland's exceptional seafood. She uses a combination of langoustines, mussels, clams and haddock but these can be swapped out for other seafood depending on availability. To prepare the soup in advance, cook the fish in the soup, remove it, then add it back in when you're ready to serve.

Rouille Combine the potato, spices, hazelnuts and garlic in a small saucepan. Add enough fish stock to just cover the potatoes then top with a lid. Bring to a simmer then cook until the potatoes are soft, about 15 minutes.

Transfer everything to a blender and add the red pepper. Blend until smooth, then transfer to a bowl and gradually whisk in the olive oil. Season with lemon juice and salt to taste. Set aside.

Fish soup Melt the butter and a dash of olive oil in a large, deep saucepan over a medium heat. Add the celery, carrots and onion with a pinch of salt. Cover the pan with a lid and sweat the vegetables for 10-15 minutes, or until soft but not coloured.

Add the garlic, tomatoes and courgette and cook for a further 5 minutes uncovered, then add the spices and cook for 5 minutes more. Add the potatoes and stir them into the other vegetables, then cook for 10 minutes. Add enough fish stock to cover, then place a lid on the pan. Bring the stock to a simmer and cook for 15 minutes more.

Add the two haddocks, langoustines and squid to the pan one at a time in the order listed, waiting 2 minutes between each addition. Add the clams and mussels then put a lid on the pan and cook for a few minutes more, or until all the mussel and clam shells have opened. Discard any which haven't opened.

To serve Serve the fish soup with the rouille and a wedge of lemon on the side.

Lorna McNee

One of Scotland's brightest talents, Lorna McNee's ingredient-led, innovative and elegant cooking style has deservedly earned her praise. She is the only female Scottish chef to hold a Michelin star, having won her first in 2021 at her Glasgow restaurant Cail Bruich.

Serves 8
4 hours
Equipment: 8 tartlet cases, 8 cm round cutter, muslin, high-powered blender

Mushroom stock
vegetable oil, as needed
2 onions, roughly chopped
2 garlic bulbs, separated into cloves
5 celery stalks, roughly chopped
2 leeks, roughly chopped
450g portobello mushrooms, sliced
300g chestnut mushrooms, sliced
300g button mushrooms, sliced
2.5 litres vegetable stock
½ bunch tarragon
½ bunch parsley
½ bunch thyme
5 white peppercorns

Filo tart
3 filo pastry sheets (30 cm × 45 cm)
120g unsalted butter, melted
100g Parmesan, grated
20g fresh thyme, leaves picked

Duxelles
600g portobello mushrooms
600g king oyster mushrooms
1 large shallot, cut into a brunoise
1 garlic clove, germ removed and microplaned
2 lemons, juiced
20g cornflour
150g double cream
10g tarragon, chopped

Black garlic gel
3g agar
100g black garlic, peeled

Lemon gel
30g sugar
3g agar
100g freshly squeezed lemon juice, strained through a fine mesh sieve

Mushroom jelly
350ml medium sweet Madeira
570ml reduced mushroom stock
9g agar

Mushroom tart

This is truly one for the mushroom lovers, using mushrooms in eight different ways, in everything from jellies to powder. There are a lot of different elements to this dish, but they can be made over two to three days.

Mushroom stock Sweat the vegetables in a large stockpot with some vegetable oil and a pinch of salt until softened, about 15 minutes. Add the portobello mushrooms and cook for a few minutes until they begin to release their water, then add the rest of the mushrooms. Cook until they have softened and released their water as well.

Add the stock and 1.5 litres water, then bring to a boil. Simmer for 1 hour, then add the herbs and peppercorns. Simmer for another hour. Remove from the heat then cover the top with a tightly fitting lid or cling film and infuse for 20 minutes.

Strain through a double layer of muslin and return to the heat, discarding the solids. Cook over high heat until reduced by half.

Filo tart Preheat the oven to 180°C.

Lay a sheet of filo pastry onto baking parchment and brush on both sides with the melted butter. Sprinkle ⅓ of the Parmesan and thyme on top of the filo, then brush another sheet with butter on both sides and lay it on top. Press down firmly so that it sticks, then sprinkle over half the remaining Parmesan and thyme. Brush the final sheet of filo on both sides, press it down firmly into the second filo later, and top with the remaining cheese and thyme.

Top the third layer of filo pastry with baking parchment and press down firmly. You can use a chopping board or oven tray to help you weigh it down evenly. Cut out 8 x 8 cm rounds of pastry from the compressed filo, then press these into the tart cases.

Bake for 10-12 minutes or until golden brown. Leave to cool in the tart cases, then remove. If there is a lot of excess butter, leave them to drain upside down on paper towels.

Duxelles Remove the gills from the portobello mushrooms and square them off. Remove the head of the king oyster and square off the body. Cut both mushrooms into a medium-sized dice, but keep them separate.

Add the shallot and garlic to a large frying pan with a pinch of salt, and sweat for 5 minutes, or until the shallot begins to soften. Add the king oyster mushrooms and cook for 2 minutes, then add the portobello mushrooms and cook for 4 minutes.

Deglaze with the lemon juice, then add the cornflour and mix. Add the cream, bring to a simmer, then remove from the heat.

Truffle sauce
1 shallot, finely sliced
1 garlic clove, finely sliced
60g button mushrooms, sliced
4 tbsp white wine
4 tbsp Madeira
200ml reduced mushroom stock
200ml double cream
100ml truffle juice
20g Parmesan, grated
30g unsalted butter, diced
½ a lemon, juiced
10g preserved black truffle, grated

Hen-of-the-woods mushrooms
100g hen-of-the-woods mushrooms
dash of oil
reduced mushroom stock,
as needed
2 tbsp unsalted butter

To serve
micro button mushrooms
cep powder
olive oil
edible flowers
fresh truffle

Black garlic gel Add the agar, black garlic, 2g salt and 200g cold water to a small saucepan and whisk together. If you are using agar flakes, soak them in the water for 15-30 minutes before bringing to a simmer. If you are using agar powder it can be simmered straight away.

Bring the pan to a boil and simmer until the agar is completely dissolved, whisking constantly, about 5 minutes. Blend the mixture until smooth, then transfer to a container to set.

Lemon gel Whisk the sugar, agar, lemon and 100g water together in a small saucepan, and follow the instructions as above for the black garlic gel.

Mushroom jelly Add the Madeira to a saucepan and simmer over a high heat until it has reduced by half. Add to the mushroom stock, then whisk in the agar. If using agar flakes, leave them to soak for 15-30 minutes. If using powder, simmer immediately.

Bring the mixture to the boil and cook for 5 minutes, or until the agar has dissolved. Strain through a chinois or fine sieve onto a wide, flat tray with a rim. Set at room temperature then chill.

Once set, cut out rings of jelly with the 8 cm round cutter, and store the pieces between baking parchment in the fridge.

Truffle sauce Sweat the garlic and shallot in a pan with some vegetable oil and a pinch of salt, but don't let them colour. Add the mushrooms and cook until they release their water. Add the white wine and cook until it has reduced to a syrup.

Add the Madeira, cook until reduced by half, then do the same with the mushroom stock. Add the cream and reduce by ⅓.

Add the truffle juice and preserved truffle, then remove from the heat and add the Parmesan. Add the diced butter in 2 batches, while blending the sauce with a high-powered blender. Taste, and season with lemon juice and more truffle if needed.

Hen-of-the-woods mushrooms Tear the clump of mushrooms into bite-sized pieces, leaving a little bit of the root attached.

Heat a dash of oil in a pan over medium-high heat and add the mushrooms. Cook until beginning to brown. Add the butter and a dash of stock to emulsify. Cook until the mushrooms are glazed.

To serve Blend the lemon and black garlic gels until smooth and transfer to a piping bag. Reheat the duxelles with a dash of cream if needed, and add the tarragon. Adjust the seasoning as needed.

Fill a tart case with this mix, and top with 5 dots of black garlic gel. Top with a piece of hen-of-the-woods.

Grate over some fresh truffle, then cover with a circle of mushroom jelly. Put 5 dots of lemon gel on top.

Slice the button mushrooms thinly and dust with some cep powder, a dot of olive oil and a pinch of salt. Top each tart with three slices of mushroom and some edible flowers.

Use a dot of black garlic gel to secure each tart to the plate. Just before serving, pour the truffle sauce around each tart.

Harriet Mansell

Over the course of her career, Harriet Mansell has developed an obsession with wild food. This means that her highly seasonal dishes are usually dictated by what she can find growing around her in Lyme Regis, where she runs restaurant and wine bar Lilac.

Serves 6
6 hours, plus time for the lamb to brine overnight
Equipment: Barbecue,
10 cm round cutter

Pickled alexanders buds
100g caster sugar
120g white wine vinegar
75g alexanders buds

Lamb brine
8 star anise
1 tbsp cumin seeds
1 tbsp black peppercorns
50g sugar

Barbecued lamb
1.5kg rolled lamb shoulder or belly
olive oil, for rubbing
smoked soy sauce, to taste
lemon juice, to taste

Barbecued greens
300g Tenderstem broccoli or kale sprouts
75ml olive oil
1 tbsp smoked soy sauce
squeeze of lemon juice

Spiced butter
1 tsp cumin seeds
1 tsp five-spice powder
150g salted butter, melted

Activated charcoal tortilla
250g wholemeal flour
25g activated charcoal powder
1 tbsp olive oil

Alexanders mayonnaise
2 egg yolks
1 tsp Dijon mustard
½ a lemon, juiced
200ml mild-flavoured olive oil
75g Alexanders leaves, roughly chopped
1 garlic clove, minced

Barbecued lamb, alexanders, rhubarb and kale tostada

This lamb tostada recipe from Harriet Mansell is served with pickled alexanders buds, a coastal flowering plant that looks and tastes a little like celery. If you can't find alexanders, other herb buds such as chive buds make a good substitute in the pickle, and lovage can replace the leaves in the mayonnaise.

Pickled alexanders buds Warm through all the ingredients except the buds with 30g salt and 50g water over a medium heat, until the salt and sugar have dissolved. Set aside to cool.

Once cool, pour the brine over the alexanders buds and store in the fridge until ready to serve. They can be used straight away, but are even better the next day.

Lamb brine Toast the star anise, cumin seeds and peppercorns in a dry frying pan until fragrant. Add them to a large pan with 2 litres of water, 100g salt and the sugar, then heat until the salt and sugar have dissolved. Set aside to cool. Once cool, add the lamb and leave in the fridge overnight to brine.

Barbecued lamb When ready to cook the lamb, prepare the barbecue or preheat the oven to 150°C. In the restaurant the lamb is cooked on a ceramic barbecue with a lid, to make it easier to control the temperature.

Remove the lamb from the brine and pat dry. Rub the lamb with olive oil and 1 teaspoon flaky sea salt.

Sear the lamb over a high heat on all sides, either on the barbecue or in a frying pan. Once the barbecue or oven is at 150°C, add the lamb and cook for 4-5 hours. The meat should be tender enough to flake with a fork once cooked.

Barbecued greens Add more fuel to the barbecue until it is hot, but not so hot that you will incinerate the greens.

Cook the greens on the barbecue for a few minutes, turning regularly, until softened and nicely charred. Remove the greens from the barbecue and dress with smoked soy sauce, salt, oil and lemon juice to taste. Set aside until ready to serve.

Spiced butter Toast the cumin seeds in a dry frying pan until just fragrant, about 30 seconds, then add the five-spice. Lightly toast for a couple of seconds then remove the spices from the heat and add them to the melted butter with an extra pinch of salt.

Activated charcoal tortilla Combine all the ingredients for the charcoal tortilla in a large bowl with 1 teaspoon flaky sea salt annd 150ml water and mix until just combined.

Roll out the dough on a lightly floured surface until it is 1 mm thick. Cut out the tortillas using a 10 cm cutter, then transfer to a tray

Poached rhubarb
3 rhubarb stalks, cut into 8-10 cm pieces
150g caster sugar

Kale crisps
200g cavolo nero or sea beet leaves
olive oil, for drizzling

Fried nettles
handful of nettle leaves
vegetable oil, for deep-frying

lined with baking parchment. Heat a dry frying pan over a medium-high heat and toast the tortillas on either side for 20 seconds, or until lightly browned.

Wrap the tortillas in baking parchment or a clean tea towel to keep warm.

Cut all the tortillas in half, then brush them with the spiced butter. Set aside until you are ready to bake them.

Alexanders mayonnaise Whisk together the egg yolks, Dijon mustard and lemon juice. Slowly emulsify in half of the oil, whisking drop by drop then building to a steady stream as the it thickens.

Blend together the remaining olive oil, alexanders and minced garlic until smooth. Slowly emulsify the herb oil into the mayonnaise. Whisk in 1 teaspoon flaky sea salt, and then taste. It should be bright, zingy and well seasoned. Add more garlic, lemon juice or salt as needed.

Poached rhubarb Place the rhubarb into a container that is not much bigger than the volume of the rhubarb, so that it can be completely submerged in the simple syrup.

Warm the sugar and 100g water over a medium heat. Cook the syrup until the sugar has dissolved, and it is just beginning to boil.

Pour the piping hot syrup over the rhubarb and immediately cover with a lid. Set aside to cool.

Once cooled, slice the rhubarb – which should still have some crunch – into 3 cm long, 0.5 cm thick pieces. Place these back in the syrup, and store in the fridge until ready to serve.

Kale crisps Preheat the oven to 170°C.

Pull the leaves off the woody rib, and tear them into small pieces. Place on an oven tray and drizzle with oil. Bake for around 10 minutes, or until they are completely crisp and dry.

Season lightly with salt and set aside.

Fried nettles Heat 2-3 cm oil in a saucepan to 150°C.

Add the nettle leaves to the oil a couple at a time. Careful, as they will still have their sting and will splutter once they touch the oil. Remove the nettles from the oil once they stop bubbling, and place on a kitchen towel-lined plate to absorb the oil.

Use tweezers to gently unfurl any leaves which have curled up, and season with a pinch of salt.

To serve Preheat the oven to 170°C.

Slice or shred the lamb into small pieces, and transfer to a bowl with all its juices. Season with a touch of smoked soy sauce, lemon juice and a pinch of salt if it needs it, and mix together.

Bake the tortillas in the oven for a couple of minutes until crisp.

Place 2 halves of tortilla on a plate and squeeze over the mayo. Add a few pickles, some lamb and a couple of pieces of rhubarb. Top with the barbecued broccoli, crispy kale and fried nettles.

Over the course of his six years spent as chef director of London's much-adored Barrafina restaurants, Angel Zapata Martin became something of a figurehead for Spanish tapas in the UK. Never straying too far from tradition – his predominant mission being to accurately recreate the tapas served in his hometown of Barcelona – Angel continually elevated his dishes to a Michelin-starred standard by using a combination of the finest Spanish and British produce available. Alongside Barrafina, Angel was also the driving force behind Spanish grill concept Parrillan when it first launched. In 2023 he returned to live with his family in Catalonia.

Angel Zapata Martin

**Above: Angel carefully plates
his anchovy and onion tart
in the kitchen of Barrafina
Borough Yards.**

Below: Edible flowers are
used to bring delicate sprays
of colour to the plate.

Serves 4-6
4 hours 30 minutes
Equipment: Mandoline

Confit shallots
5 shallots, peeled
olive oil, to cover

Suckling pig confit
olive oil, to cover the meat
1 bay leaf
1 head of garlic, halved
1 guindilla chilli
1 small sprig of sage
1 clove
1 tsp juniper berries
1 tsp cumin seeds
200g suckling pig leg
1 suckling pig rack of ribs
1 suckling pig head, cut in half
1 suckling pig shoulder
1.5 tbsp confit shallots

Suckling pig croquetas
dash of oil, for cooking
180ml whole milk
½ tbsp confit shallots
a pinch of cumin
20g flour
22g butter
3 eggs, beaten
panko breadcrumbs, for coating

Suckling pig sauce
500g rhubarb
100g sugar
a dash of oil
suckling pig bones, from above
1 head of garlic, cloves peeled
and halved
2 shallots, thinly sliced
1 carrot, thinly sliced
1 tsp tomato purée
200ml port
1 litre chicken stock
1 sprig of rosemary
1 bay leaf

Rhubarb salad
100g rhubarb, sliced into ribbons
on a mandoline
ice water
olive oil

Rhubarb chutney
500g rhubarb, diced (save the trim)
100g caster sugar
2 tbsp dried apricots
50ml Pedro Ximénez vinegar
2 tbsp shallot confit

To serve
vegetable oil, for deep-frying
leek flowers

Suckling pig and rhubarb
This ambitious springtime recipe from Angel combines suckling pig leg croquettes with pressed ribs, head and shoulder and a tart chutney. Use forced Yorkshire rhubarb, if possible.

Confit shallots Preheat the oven to 120°C.

Cover the shallots with olive oil and foil. Cook for 1 hour. Cool, then finely chop.

Suckling pig confit Preheat the oven to 95°C.

Combine the oil, herbs and spices in an oven tray, and warm to 95°C.

Season the meat and submerge in the oil. Cook the rack, head and shoulders for 2 hours, and the legs for 4.

Remove the skin from the pork in one piece and lay in a tray.

Remove the meat from the bones, except for the leg. Mix with the shallot confit and season. Top the skin with the meat, then wrap and weigh down with another tray and a weight on top. Refrigerate overnight, then portion.

Sucking pig croquetas Remove the meat from the leg in chunky pieces. Fry in olive oil until slightly crisp. Set aside.

Bring the milk, cumin and confit shallots to a simmer. Melt the butter and, once foaming, whisk in the flour. Add the milk gradually to the butter and flour, whisking until thickened. Season with salt.

Mix in the leg meat. Transfer to a tray, cool, then chill overnight.

Divide the mix into 32g portions, then coat in beaten egg and panko. Chill on a lined tray until ready to fry.

Suckling pig sauce Combine the rhubarb and sugar. Macerate for 30-45 minutes. Heat a dash of oil in a large pan, and add the pork bones. Brown on all sides. Set aside. Add the garlic, brown slightly, then add the shallots and carrots until caramelised.

Add the tomato purée. Cook for a few minutes, then deglaze with port, then add the rhubarb trimmings, sugar, stock, rosemary and bay leaf.

Bring to a simmer and cook for 30 minutes. Strain and return to the pan. Reduce until thickened to a sauce-like consistency.

Rhubarb salad Bathe the ribbons in ice water for 2 minutes. Drain, dress with olive oil and season.

Rhubarb chutney Mix the rhubarb and sugar in a pan. Leave for 30-45 minutes, until the sugar begins to dissolve. Add the remaining ingredients and cook until jammy. Set aside.

To serve Heat a few centimetres of oil to 180°C in a high-sided pan. Fry the croquettes until golden. Drain on paper towels.

Fry each portion of suckling pig confit in a pan, skin side down, until the skin is crisp.

Add a portion of suckling pig confit, a quenelle of rhubarb chutney, a croquette and some rhubarb salad to each plate. Garnish the rhubarb salad and chutney with leek flowers.

Serves 4
1 hour
Equipment: 18 cm ovenproof pan
or cake tin

Tart
12 large Tropea onions
50g butter into cubes, plus extra
melted butter for brushing
1 sprig of lemon thyme, leaves only
20 cm diameter sheet of puff pastry
icing sugar, for dusting
6 l'Escala anchovy fillets

Manzanilla olive sauce
12 olives, finely chopped and pits
reserved, plus a few extras cut in half
for garnish
a dash of olive oil
1 shallot, cut into a brunoise
1 garlic clove, minced
1 sprig of lemon thyme, stem only
10g butter
100ml brandy
200ml chicken stock

To serve
edible flowers

Tropea onion and L'Escala anchovy tart with Manzanilla olive sauce

This beautiful onion tart from Angel Zapata Martin is cooked upside down like a tarte Tatin, before being turned out and topped with salty L'Escala anchovy fillets. A sauce made from Manzanilla olives completes the dish and helps to balance out the sweetness of the charred, roasted onions. Angel recommends using M. Sureda Spanish anchovies if you can find them

Tart Blacken and char the outside of the onions either over coals on a barbecue, or under the grill. Once the skin is completely charred, wrap the onions tightly in foil until they are cool enough to handle. Peel the charred skin off the onions, then cut them in half.

Preheat the oven to 200°C.

Grease the pan and line it with baking parchment if it's not non-stick. Place the onions into the pan cut side down, arranging them so that the whole surface is covered. Dot the onions with a generous amount of butter, and sprinkle over the thyme leaves and flaky sea salt.

Lay the puff pastry over the onions, tucking it down and around the edges. Brush the pastry with melted butter, and dust lightly with icing sugar.

Bake the tart for 20-25 minutes until the pastry is cooked through and the onions are golden. Set aside to rest for a few minutes.

Manzanilla olive sauce Sauté the olives and their pits in a dash of olive oil with the shallot, garlic and the lemon thyme stem. Once the shallot begins to brown, add the butter and cook until the butter browns and smells nutty.

Deglaze the pan with brandy, and carefully flambé. Add the chicken stock and reduce until it thickens. Strain the sauce through a fine mesh sieve.

To serve Turn out the tart and garnish with the anchovies, edible flowers and reserved olive halves. Drizzle over the olive sauce.

With a background in Michelin-starred kitchens and as a leading development chef, it was no surprise that Chet Sharma's debut restaurant BiBi was quickly met with acclaim when it opened in 2021. Chet weaves British ingredients into contemporary takes on Indian dishes which are rooted in authenticity. At BiBi – meaning 'lady of the house' in Urdu, a name inspired by his grandmothers – sustainability reigns supreme; menus are led by the best market produce and the bounty of the English coast and countryside – Chet believes chefs should be able to name the boat and fishermen who catch their seafood. In his kitchen, culinary gadgets sit alongside a traditional Sigree grill.

Chet Sharma

Above: Chet plates up his violina squash purée in BiBi's sweeping open kitchen.

Top: Much of the menu at BiBi is cooked on skewers over hot coals in the Sigree grill, inspired by Chet's grandfather's memories of Lahore's kebab vendors before India's partition.

Bottom: Tokyo turnips are skewered and lightly cooked over the grill to infuse some smoke flavour. They will be used to garnish the lamb barra kebab.

Serves 4

3 hours, plus time for the fish to cure and lemon oil to infuse overnight
Equipment: Barbecue, metal skewers, blender, stick blender, muslin

Cured fish
30g caster sugar
1g ajwain (carom seed), lightly toasted
4 × 125g halibut fillets, skin-on and pin boned
ice, as needed
brown rice vinegar, as needed

Lemon oil
500g grapeseed oil
50g lemon zest, pith removed

Green chilli sauce
1kg white chicken stock
30g green chilli pickle

Violina squash purée
250g violina butternut squash, peeled and evenly diced
1g ajwain (carom seed), lightly toasted
75g brown butter, melted
brown rice vinegar, to taste

Resting butter
500g unsalted butter
100g milk powder
10g ajwain (carom seed), lightly toasted
25g lemon juice
10g katsuobushi
10g dashi concentrate

To serve
100g various sea herbs, such as sea aster, sea fennel, sea kale, sea purslane and sea beets
ice water
smoked pike roe

Green chilli halibut

This dish makes the most of halibut fillets by curing them, then blistering the skin. At BiBi, Chet cooks the fish on a Sigree grill but a home barbecue works just as well. The fish is served with green chilli sauce and a sweet squash purée, to balance the heat.

Cured fish Blitz together the sugar, 70g flaky sea salt and ajwain. Spread half the cure over a tray and top with the fish, skin-side down. Sprinkle the rest of the cure on top. Set aside for 10 minutes.

In a bowl big enough to hold a fish fillet, make an ice bath of 50% water, 50% ice. Add 2% of brown rice vinegar. For example, 250g ice, 250g water and 10ml brown rice vinegar.

Brush all of the cure off the halibut, then dip each fillet in the ice bath, remove and pat dry. Place the fillets on a wire rack, skin side up, and store in the fridge overnight.

Lemon oil Warm the oil and lemon, ensuring it doesn't get hotter than 70°C, for 15-20 minutes. Remove from the heat and stir in 10g sea salt, then let cool. Transfer to the fridge to infuse overnight.

Green chilli sauce Bring the chicken stock to a boil. Cook uncovered over high heat until the stock has reduced to 100ml. Remove from the heat, then blend in the chilli pickle with a stick blender. Season with 5g sea salt, then chill until needed.

Violina squash purée Steam the squash until tender, then transfer to a blender. Add 5g salt and ajwain and blend while hot, then stream in the brown butter until it forms a purée. Add brown rice vinegar adjust salt to taste. It should be stiff and very glossy. Add ice to loosen if it's too thick, then chill.

Resting butter Add the butter and milk powder to a pan and cook until the butter is dark golden. Remove from the heat then add the ajwain and lemon juice. Cool to 80°C. Add the katsuobushi and dashi concentrate. Cool to 50°C.

Strain through a muslin-lined sieve. Weigh the resting brown butter, and add 2% salt. Set aside until needed.

To serve Prepare a barbecue for direct grilling and skewer the fish. Warm enough brown butter to cover the fish to a temperature of 46°C.

Blanch the sea herbs separately in boiling water for ten seconds, and refresh in ice water.

Cook the fish over the coals, skin-side down – until blistered. Cook for 10-15 seconds on the other side or until just cooked. Transfer to the warm butter and rest for 10-15 minutes.

While the fish is resting, heat up the green chilli sauce and squash purée. Briefly warm all the sea herbs except the sea beets, then dress with lemon oil. Cook over coals for 10 seconds, or until the leaves just begin to change colour.

Place a tablespoon of squash purée on each plate, followed by ½ teaspoon of smoked roe. Strain the fish from the butter and place on the plate. Garnish with the remaining sea herbs, then pour over the green chilli sauce.

Serves 4
2 hours 30 minutes, plus marinating time
Equipment: Barbecue, skewers, spice grinder, blender

Lamb
4 × 200g aged lamb rumps
30g garlic + 50g ginger paste
30g lemon juice

Garam masala
5g green + 3g black cardamom pods
5g cloves
7g cinnamon + 2g cinnamon leaves
5g mace
5g rose petals
20g shahi jeera
20g cumin seeds
10g black peppercorns
5g ground ginger
1g nutmeg
1g pathar phool, (stone flower)
10g coriander seeds
4g fennel seeds
10g dried fenugreek leaves

Yoghurt marinade
500g yoghurt
35g garlic + 70g ginger paste
100g mustard oil
80g onions, blended to a paste
20g fried onions, blended to a paste
20g Kashmiri chilli powder
10g deggi mirch chilli powder

Walnut chutney
50g walnuts
10g Bombay onion
5g garlic, green germ removed
10g ginger, peeled
10g fresh coriander
5g mint leaves
5g brown rice wine vinegar
10g grapeseed oil
10g walnut oil
5g red chilli pickle
1g dried mint
20g hung yoghurt or Greek yoghurt

Green pepper sauce
50g Indian long peppers
25g poblano peppers
10g spinach
25g fresh coriander
5g mint leaves
30g tofu
2g amchoor
1g chaat masala
2g roasted cumin
25g grapeseed oil

To serve
2 quartered Tokyo turnips
chilli oil, to taste

Lamb barra kebab

Barra kebab is one of the original kebabs upon which Mughlai cuisine is based. Here, Chet takes inspiration from the burra kebabs he used to eat when visiting Delhi 6 – the area immediately around Jama Masjid in old Delhi. He serves barbecued, spiced, lamb rump with a sweet walnut ketchup and powerful pepper sauce. You'll need flaky sea salt and black salt for this recipe.

Lamb Preheat the oven to 120°C.

Remove the fat caps from the rumps. Mix together the garlic paste, ginger paste, lemon juice and 5g sea salt. Marinate the lamb in this mixture while you make the garam masala.

Garam masala Add all the garam masala spices to a baking tray and toast in the oven for around 20 minutes, or until lightly coloured and aromatic. Cool and grind to a powder.

Yoghurt marinade Combine all the ingredients with 20g sea salt, 50g garam masala, and the lamb. Leave to marinate for at least 4 hours, or overnight.

Walnut chutney Preheat the oven to 165°C.

Roast the walnuts for 8 minutes, or until lightly golden. Rub the walnuts with a clean tea towel to remove the bitter skins.

Blend the walnuts with 50g water, then add the remaining chutney ingredients except the yoghurt and blend again. Transfer to a container and, once cool, whisk in the yoghurt by hand to avoid splitting. Season with black salt and chill.

Green pepper sauce Heat up a few centimetres of oil to 180°C. Deep-fry the peppers for 2 minutes, then remove and drain on paper towels. Allow to cool then peel the skin off.

Boil a pot of lightly salted water and blanch the spinach, coriander and mint for 30 seconds. Shock in ice water.

Squeeze all the water out of the blanched greens and blend with the skinned peppers. Add the tofu, 20g ice, spices, 1g sea salt and 1g black salt. Blend until smooth, then stream in the grapeseed oil while the blender is running. Adjust the seasoning to taste and refrigerate until needed.

To serve Prepare a barbecue for direct grilling. Skewer the lamb rumps and cook over the coals, then remove from the barbecue and let rest. The lamb will continue to cook as it rests. For rare lamb, take it off the barbecue once it reaches 48°C. It should register 52-55°C after resting.

While the lamb rests, dress the turnips and turnip leaves in the chilli oil, then barbecue the turnips and turnip leaves separately over high heat. The turnips should be charred and the leaves lightly cooked.

Add some walnut chutney to each plate, then add two spoonfuls of green pepper sauce to the plate for the lamb to sit on. Carve the lamb and season with salt, then place on top of the green pepper sauce. Add some turnips and turnip tops to each plate.

Michelle Trusselle

With years of experience behind her working in classical fine dining kitchens, Michelle Trusselle is now blazing her own trail at her London-based supper club concept Myristica, where she's on a mission to celebrate the Caribbean flavours she fell in love with as a child.

Serves 8
1 hour 30 minutes, plus freezing time

Sweet potato and quinoa croquettes
600g whole sweet potatoes
160g red and white quinoa
1 spring onion, cut in half
5 garlic cloves, 1 whole, 4 minced
12 thyme sprigs
2 tbsp olive oil
2 onions, finely chopped
¼ Scotch bonnet chilli, finely chopped
4 tsp jerk seasoning
2 tbsp fresh coriander, chopped
250g panko breadcrumbs
3 eggs, beaten
250g plain flour
vegetable oil, for deep frying

Pink grapefruit-dressed butterhead lettuce salad
1 head of butterhead lettuce
1 pink grapefruit, juiced
4 tbsp olive oil
2 tsp honey
1 tsp Dijon mustard

Paprika mayonnaise
150g mayonnaise
1 tsp smoked paprika

Sweet potato and quinoa croquettes, paprika mayonnaise, pink grapefruit-dressed butterhead lettuce

These sweet and spiced croquettes are fried until irresistibly crisp and served with a pink grapefruit-dressed butterhead salad. They make an elegant starter, and the croquettes can be made in advance and fried from frozen before serving.

Croquettes Preheat the oven to 180°C.

Roast the sweet potato whole for 1 hour, or until soft.

Simmer the quinoa with 750ml water, some salt, spring onion, whole garlic clove and 6 thyme sprigs for 15 minutes, until just cooked.

Strain the quinoa and remove the aromatics, then rinse with cold water and set aside to drain.

Fry the onions in the olive oil over medium-low heat for 8-10 minutes, until translucent. Add the minced garlic, Scotch bonnet and remaining thyme. Cook for 2 minutes, until the garlic is fragrant and the chilli soft. Add the jerk seasoning and cook for 1 minute.

Peel the skin off the sweet potato, and transfer to a bowl. Mash, then add the onion mixture and 300g of the drained quinoa. Mix again, then add the fresh coriander and season with salt if needed. Transfer the mixture to the freezer, briefly, to firm up.

Roll the mixture into 70g balls. Transfer the croquettes to a tray lined with baking parchment. Freeze until solid, about 2 hours.

Meanwhile, mix the panko breadcrumbs with 160g of the remaining cooked quinoa.

Once the croquettes are solid, prepare three bowls, one with the flour, one with the egg and one with the panko and quinoa mix. Coat the croquettes with the flour, then the egg and finally the panko and quinoa. Transfer to the fridge until ready to fry.

Pink grapefruit-dressed butterhead lettuce salad Tear the washed and dried butterhead lettuce leaves into large pieces.

Whisk together the pink grapefruit juice, olive oil, honey and Dijon mustard and season with salt to taste.

To serve Heat the vegetable oil to 170°C in a high-sided pan.

Fry the croquettes until golden brown on both sides, then drain on kitchen towels.

Combine the smoked paprika and mayonnaise. Dress the butterhead lettuce leaves in the pink grapefruit dressing.

Serve the croquettes with the lettuce and paprika mayonnaise.

Having honed her craft under the likes of Angela Hartnett and Clare Smyth, Pip Lacey was quickly identified as a rising star of the restaurant world. Her unrelenting drive to be at the top of her game paid off when she became head chef at the Michelin-starred Murano, before, in 2018, forging her own path with the opening of woodfire-focused Hicce in Kings Cross and, later, Islington pub Hicce Hart. At both, Pip's classical training is balanced with an accomplished simplicity that gives the finest seasonal British ingredients space to shine – a relaxed, confident style which is mirrored by the convivial atmosphere of her restaurants.

Pip Lacey

Left: A rich, dark muscovado sugar is used to flavour the crème caramel.

Right: Grated courgette is dusted with flour. It will be deep fried into feather-light kakiage.

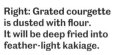

Above: Pip's eighty-cover
restaurant Hicce benefits
from a large, open pass
and counter seating,
so customers can watch
the action as their
food is prepared.

Serves 4
1 hour

Mayonnaise
2 egg yolks
1 tbsp Dijon mustard
1 tsp rice vinegar
250g vegetable oil
½ a lemon, juiced
½ a lime, juiced
a pinch of cayenne pepper

Kakiage
2 green courgettes
3 white onions, sliced 3 mm thick
1 tsp nigella seeds
vegetable oil, for deep-frying
400g gluten-free self-raising flour,
plus more for dusting
300g lager
300g sparkling water

Courgette and onion kakiage, citrus mayo, cayenne

Kakiage is a style of tempura that uses chopped up vegetables coated in a light batter. Pip tosses her courgette and onion version with nigella seeds and fries until golden, before serving them with a citrusy mayonnaise and a dusting of cayenne pepper for a touch of heat.

Mayonnaise Whisk the egg yolk, mustard, and vinegar together. Slowly add the oil drop by drop while whisking until the mixture begins to thicken. Pour the oil in a steady stream until it is all incorporated. Add the citrus juices and a pinch of salt. When ready to serve, dust the mayonnaise with a pinch of cayenne pepper.

Kakiage Grate the courgettes on the large side of a box grater. Mix together the courgette, onion and nigella seeds.

Heat up a few centimetres of oil in a high-sided saucepan to 170°C. Whisk together the gluten-free flour, lager and water.

Take a handful of the courgette and onion mix and transfer to a small bowl. Add a pinch of flour and mix it all together. Using a small ladle, add a spoonful of batter, mix briefly, then use tongs to add the battered veg to the hot oil. Fry for a few minutes, or until golden brown and crisp.

Drain the kakiage on paper towels, season with salt, and repeat with the remaining vegetables.

To serve Plate the kakiage with the mayonnaise on the side.

Serves 6
1 hour 30 minutes, plus chilling time
Equipment: 6 × 180ml moulds

Muscovado caramel
100g caster sugar
100g dark muscovado sugar

Crème caramel
397g milk
1 × 397g tin of condensed milk
4 Italian eggs, beaten

Crème caramel

Pip's take on this classic dessert uses a combination of caster and dark muscovado sugar to give an even deeper flavour to the caramel. Make sure to leave yourself ample time to allow your crème caramels to chill once they're out of the oven.

Muscovado caramel Bring all the ingredients to a boil in a high-sided pan with 120g water. Cook over medium heat until the caramel comes to a boil.

Prepare your moulds so that they are ready for the caramel.

When the caramel comes to temperature, remove the pan from the heat and immediately pour a layer of about 2 cm of caramel into the moulds. Be extremely careful when pouring the caramel, keeping your hands well out of the way. Allow to cool.

Crème caramel Preheat the oven to 150°C, no fan.

Bring the milk to a boil, then add the condensed milk and whisk until well combined. Transfer the eggs to a bowl, then pour the milk mixture over the eggs, whisking constantly, until the milk and eggs are combined. Strain the mixture through a fine mesh sieve and set aside.

Slowly pour the milk mixture over the caramel. Place the moulds in a high-sided tray and fill it 1 cm deep with water to make a double boiler.

Cook the crème caramel for 15 minutes – the egg mix should be mostly set but still have some jiggle. If they are still liquid, give them a few more minutes.

To serve Remove the moulds from the oven, then place them in the fridge for at least 2 hours. Use a plate to turn each crème caramel out and serve chilled.

Nina Matsunaga

At her and husband James' Lake District gastropub The Black Bull, Nina Matsunaga combines local produce with pan-Asian flavours and techniques to create a punchy menu of dishes that you wouldn't necessarily expect from a country pub.

Serves 4-6
6 hours, plus time for the kimchi to ferment
Equipment: Jar for kimchi

Kimchi
1 napa cabbage, core removed and roughly chopped
1 medium carrot, julienned
2 tbsp brown rice flour
120g fish sauce
50g gochugaru
2 tbsp caster sugar
2 tbsp sesame seeds
4 garlic cloves, minced
3 cm piece of ginger, grated

Cured egg yolk
175ml soy sauce
2 tbsp mirin
4 egg yolks

Fish sauce caramel
175ml fish sauce
4 tbsp brown sugar
8 tbsp palm sugar
4 tbsp raw honey
8 garlic cloves
2 chunks of galangal, sliced
8 lemongrass stalks, chopped
2 Thai chillies, left whole
2 dried Thai chillies

Beef rump and pastrami
800g beef rump
200g pastrami

Takikomi gohan
300g Japanese short grain rice
3 dried shiitake mushrooms, soaked in warm water for 30 minutes
1 small carrot, julienned
360ml dashi
2 tbsp mirin
2 tbsp soy sauce

Fish sauce caramel-glazed beef rump with takikomi gohan, kimchi, pastrami and soy-cured egg yolk

Nina pairs Japanese takikomi gohan with tender pastrami, fizzing kimchi and a fish sauce caramel so good you'll want to make a triple batch. Homemade kimchi makes this dish extra special, but you could use a good quality shop-bought version to save time.

Kimchi Dissolve 250g salt in 1.2 litres of water. Add the carrot and cabbage, mix well, then soak for 1 hour.

Add 250g water and the flour to a pan. Whisk until dissolved, then add the fish sauce, gochugaru, sugar, sesame seeds, garlic and ginger. Simmer for a few minutes, until thickened, stirring frequently.

Rinse and drain the vegetables and mix with the kimchi sauce.

Pack into a jar, using a weight or sandwich bag of water to ensure everything is submerged. Ferment for 4-6 weeks.

Burp the kimchi daily for 2 weeks, then every 2-3 days for the next 2 weeks. After that it won't need burping often. After 4 weeks, taste it. If it's too salty leave it for another 2 weeks.

Once you're happy, remove the weight and store in the fridge.

Cured egg yolk Combine the soy sauce and mirin. Add the yolks and refrigerate. Cure for at least 6 hours, but no more than 14.

Fish sauce caramel Bring all the ingredients to a boil, then cook over medium-high heat for 20 minutes, until thickened. Strain.

Beef rump Preheat the oven to 180°C. Season the beef on all sides with salt, then sear it hard.

Transfer to an oven tray and roast 15-20 minutes, glazing halfway with some caramel. Remove from the oven when it is 35-38°C in the centre. Glaze with more caramel once cooked.

Wrap in foil and rest at room temperature for 20-30 minutes.

Takikomi gohan Wash the rice 3 times, until the water mostly runs clear. Drain the mushrooms, then thinly slice. Transfer the takikomi gohan ingredients to a heavy saucepan or donabe, and bring to a simmer. Cover, then turn the heat to medium-low and cook for 15-20 minutes, until all the liquid has been absorbed. Turn off the heat and let the rice sit, covered for 20 minutes.

Use a rice paddle or wooden spoon to fluff up the takikomi gohan.

To serve Fry the pastrami on all sides until crisp. Thinly slice.

Slice the beef, then drizzle with its juices and caramel. Top the rice with the beef, pastrami and yolk, and serve kimchi alongside.

American-born Jun Tanaka learned his craft alongside some of the best chefs in the world, honing his skills in London's top fine dining restaurants. He puts that rigorous classical training to good use at his Michelin-starred restaurant The Ninth in Fitzrovia, which opened in 2015 as his first solo venture. There, he serves exquisite, French-led small plates with a hefty Mediterranean influence, specialising in raw and cured dishes, as well as chargrilled meat and fish. Despite being awarded its first star just a year after opening, it has remained a remarkably relaxed neighbourhood spot, loved by locals.

Jun Tanaka

Below: A Sardinian artichoke is trimmed of its tough outer leaves ahead of deep-frying.

Above: Jun tends to a pot
in the kitchen of his
Michelin-starred restaurant,
The Ninth.
Right: A Sardinian artichoke
is gently lowered into the
fryer and cooked at 120°C
for a perfect crispy finish.

Serves 6

3 hours, plus overnight freezing time
Equipment: Blender

Herb oil
600ml grapeseed oil
50g chives
50g parsley
50g tarragon
ice water, as needed

Artichokes
6 spiky Sardinian artichokes
lemon juice
vegetable oil, for deep-frying

Herb aioli
3 egg yolks, from eggs boiled
for 7 minutes
3 egg yolks, raw
50g Dijon mustard
40g lemon juice
25g white wine vinegar

Crispy artichokes, herb aioli

This striking dish of crispy, deep-fried artichokes is elevated by the addition of a verdant green aioli, emulsified using a herb oil made from scratch. You can either plate this up as individual starters or serve as part of a sharing platter.

Herb oil Heat the grapeseed oil to 70°C and prepare a bowl of ice water. Place all the herbs in a blender and blend with the hot oil until smooth, taking great care not to fill the blender more than ⅓ of the way up. In the restaurant this would be done for 6 minutes, but this can burn out the motor of domestic blenders so take care and blend in stages if needed. Make sure there is a way for steam to escape from the blender, and cover the steam vent with a tea towel to protect your hands.

Pour the oil into a bowl, then set it over the bowl of ice water. Chill the herb oil, then pour it into a container. Freeze the herb oil overnight.

The next day, the oil will have separated from the solids. Pour off the green oil into a new container and discard the solids.

Artichokes Remove the outer leaves from the artichokes. Trim the stem to around 10 cm in length. Peel the stem and then cut the top off the artichokes. Keep the finished artichokes in water with some lemon juice to prevent them from oxidising. Once they are all prepared, take them out of the water and dry them on paper towels.

Heat up the vegetable oil to 120°C and deep-fry the artichokes for around 20 minutes, or until cooked through. Drain the artichokes on paper towels, then leave to cool in the fridge. Reserve the oil for the second fry.

Herb aioli While the artichokes cool, make the aioli. Add all the ingredients to a blender. Measure out 500ml of the herb oil. Start the blender and slowly pour in the herb oil until it emulsifies. Season to taste with salt.

To serve Reheat the artichoke oil to 180°C. Carefully open up the leaves of the cooled artichokes. Deep-fry for 3 minutes or until golden brown. Drain on paper towels then season with flaky sea salt. Serve with the herb aioli.

Serves 4
3 hours, plus soaking
and infusion time
Equipment: Blender

4 × 300g turbot tranches (ask your
fishmonger to prepare these)
50g butter, plus extra for
cooking vegetables
400g variegated kale, blanched
100g monk's beard

Lovage oil
250ml grapeseed oil
75g lovage, roughly chopped
ice

Pickling liquor
250ml white wine vinegar
1 bunch of dill
90g caster sugar

Pickled cockles
1kg cockles, washed very well and
soaked in water overnight
olive oil
2 shallots, finely sliced
1 garlic clove, finely sliced
1 sprig of thyme
200ml white wine

Fish stock
olive oil
1 stick of celery, cut into 1cm pieces
1 onion, cut into 1cm pieces
1 leek, cut into 1cm pieces
½ bulb fennel, cut into 1cm pieces
1 garlic clove
1 sprig of thyme
5g black peppercorns
2 slices of lemon
½ bunch of parsley
250ml white wine
1kg white fish bones

Vin jaune sauce
2 shallots, finely sliced
2 garlic, finely sliced
olive oil, for cooking
1 sprig of thyme
1 bay leaf
100ml dry vermouth
100ml vin jaune
150ml cockle juice
150ml fish stock
75g unsalted butter, cut into
small cubes
½ lemon

Roast turbot, pickled cockles, kale and vin jaune sauce

Jun compliments the majestic flavour of turbot with a sauce combining vin jaune, vermouth and dill-pickled cockles in this luxurious, classically-grounded dish. Variegated kale and dots of lovage oil bring further colour and freshness to the plate. Pre-made fish stock can be used to save time.

Lovage oil Heat the grapeseed oil in a pan until it reaches 80°C.

Carefully add the hot oil and lovage to a blender and blend on high for 6 mins or until completely smooth. Make sure there is a way for steam to escape from the blender, and cover the steam vent with a tea towel to protect your hands.

Transfer the oil to a bowl and chill over ice. Once cold, transfer to a container then leave to infuse overnight.

Pickled cockles To make the pickling liquor, place the vinegar, dill and sugar into a pan with 50g salt and 500ml water and bring to the boil. Set aside to cool.

Sweat the shallots, garlic and thyme in olive oil for 2 minutes. Add the cockles and wine, then cover and cook for 2 minutes, or until the cockles open. Drain the cockles in a colander on top of a pan or bowl to collect the juice. Pick the meat from the shells and strain the cockle juice through a very fine sieve.

Pickle the cockles in the pickling liquor for 2.5 hours.

Fish stock Sweat the celery, onion, leek and fennel in plenty of olive oil for 5 minutes, keeping the heat low so that the vegetables don't colour. Add the garlic, thyme, peppercorns, lemon, parsley and white wine and turn the heat up to medium. Reduce the wine until it has almost completely evaporated then add the fish bones, cover with 2 litres water and bring to a simmer. Cook for 20 minutes, skimming as necessary.

Vin jaune sauce While the cockles pickle, make the vin jaune sauce. Sweat the shallots, garlic, thyme and bay leaf in olive oil for 2 minutes. Add the vin jaune and vermouth and simmer until reduced by half. Add the fish stock and reserved cockle juice and reduce by half again. Pass the sauce through a fine sieve.

Warm up the vin jaune sauce in a small saucepan and add the cold butter a few pieces at a time, whisking as you go, until it is all emulsified into the sauce. Add lemon juice and salt to taste.

To serve Preheat the oven to 200°C.

Heat an oven-proof frying pan and add a dash of olive oil. Season the turbot tranches with salt and place in the pan, skin side down. Cook the turbot for 3 minutes until the skin is crisp then flip over. Add the butter and transfer to the oven. Cook for 10-12 minutes, basting every few minutes with the butter. Remove from the oven and rest for 2 minutes.

Heat some more butter in a pan and add the kale and monk's beard. Cook for a couple of minutes, then season with salt.

Place the turbot onto four plates, then place a few leaves of kale next to each piece of fish. Spoon the cockles over each piece, followed by some monk's beard. Spoon the vin jaune sauce over the fish and dot around the herb oil.

One of the most prominent chefs and restaurateurs in the South West, Peter Sanchez-Iglesias first burst onto the scene when he and his brother Jonray took over their parents' neighbourhood trattoria Casamia in the Bristol suburb of Westbury-on-Trym and gradually transformed it into an ambitious, award-winning restaurant. He's since gone on to relocate and reconceptualise Casamia – now called Casa – as a more informal Italian restaurant, as well as opening other spots including the lauded Paco Tapas. Named after his father, this Michelin-starred tapas bar harks back to Peter's Spanish heritage, blending modernity with tradition to create a little slice of Andalusia in the heart of Bristol, all whilst showcasing the finest British produce around.

Peter Sanchez-Iglesias

Left: At Paco Tapas, Peter celebrates the food of Andalusia, where his father grew up.

Left: Peter's elevated take on a traditional tortilla fast became a staple of the Paco Tapas menu.

Above: Perfectly crisped potatoes form the core of this Michelin-starred Spanish omelette.

Serves 4
2 hours 30 minutes, plus time
for the mixture to soak
Equipment: 12 cm blini pan,
mandoline

3-4 large chipping potatoes
vegetable oil, for deep-frying
2 eggs
2 egg yolks
½ a white onion
drizzle of extra virgin olive oil

Tortilla Española

There are few dishes more representative of Spanish cuisine than the humble tortilla and this recipe shows the amount of work necessary to take a classic to Michelin-starred level. Peter fries the potatoes at two different temperatures to achieve the perfect crisp finish, allowing them to soak in the egg mixture for up to three days before frying.

Potatoes Heat oil for deep frying to 120°C. You want to have plenty of space for frying but enough room left to ensure it won't boil over.

Peel the potatoes and slice them to the thickness of a pound coin. Wash very well in cold water to remove excess starch. Drain the potatoes very thoroughly and pat dry.

Fry the potatoes in small batches for 5 minutes, or until soft. Drain on paper towels.

Beat together the whole eggs with the yolks. Slice the onion to the same thickness as the potatoes.

Once your potatoes are all cooked through, heat the oil to 170°C.

Carefully add your cooked potatoes back to the oil in small batches. Cook until crisp but not coloured, mixing to ensure even cooking – 1-2 minutes. Drain well on paper towels and repeat with the remaining batches.

Once the potatoes are cooked, chop into small pieces while hot. They should be around 1 cm in size but this can be very rustic.

Weigh out 110g of the egg mixture and add 80g of chopped crispy potatoes. Mix this thoroughly and leave to soak.

Onions Heat the oil to 170°C. Add the sliced onions to the oil in small batches and fry until dark golden brown, stirring frequently.

Once the onions are golden, drain on paper towels. They should be slightly crispy. Leave to cool for a couple of minutes, then add 15g to the egg and potato mix with 2g sea salt. Mix thoroughly with a spoon ensuring all the potato and onion is submerged. Let this sit for 1 hour or up to 3 days in the fridge.

After 1 hour, the mixture should have thickened significantly. You will need to add a small amount of your remaining egg mixture to loosen it up before cooking. We often describe the desired consistency as mayonnaise: thick but not dry, and slightly loose.

Tortilla Preheat the blini pan on a medium heat with a dash of olive oil, then wipe the pan dry with a paper towel. You should have a light layer of oil all around the pan.

Turn the egg mixture out into the pan and use a spoon to level it out. You should hear a gentle sizzle when adding the mixture. You want the pan to be full to the brim but also flat and even.

Turn the heat down as low as possible and cook for 1 minute 30 seconds. Once cooked, turn the tortilla out onto a small side plate which has been greased lightly with olive oil. Return to the heat and add the tortilla back to the pan wet side down. Use a spoon to push down any flaps you may get. Cook for a further 1 and a half minutes on low to seal the centre. Turn the tortilla over in the pan again and leave to rest for 5 minutes, then serve.

Makes 25-30 croquetas
1 hour 30 minutes, plus time for the milk to infuse and the béchamel to firm up

Infusion
550g whole milk
280g sliced serrano ham, cut into 0.5 cm pieces

Leeks
100g salted butter
40g white leek, finely chopped

Béchamel
90g flour, plus extra for dusting
75g mature Manchego, grated
a pinch of nutmeg

To serve
3 eggs, beaten
panko, for dusting
vegetable oil, for frying

Jamón croquetas

Two of Spain's best-known ingredients, serrano ham and Manchego, are used in Peter's simple croquetas recipe. By allowing the jamón to infuse in the milk, the saltiness permeates through the entire mixture, ensuring that the croquetas are packed full of flavour.

Infusion Bring the milk to a simmer and add 120g of the serrano ham. Remove from the heat and leave to infuse for at least 3 hours prior to cooking.

After 3 hours, strain the ham from the milk, discarding the ham.

Leeks Heat the milk infusion to just below the boil and melt the butter in a frying pan. Sweat the finely chopped leeks for 2-3 minutes, but don't let them colour. Add the remaining chopped ham, then cook for a further 2 minutes until the fat renders out.

Béchamel Add the flour and cook for a further 2 minutes, stirring constantly, then slowly start adding the warm milk in stages until you have a nice, thick sauce. You might need slightly more or less than 550g milk to get the right consistency. Stir in the Manchego and season with a pinch of grated nutmeg and black pepper. Transfer the mixture to a container and leave to cool in the fridge overnight.

The next day, divide the set mixture into 35g portions on a lightly floured tray, using two spoons to quenelle them. Lightly dust the quenelles with more flour, then roll them into ovals with your hands.

To serve Prepare a bowl of beaten egg and a bowl of panko breadcrumbs. Dip the croquetas into the beaten eggs then toss them in the panko breadcrumbs to ensure an even coating.

Heat oil for deep frying to a temperature of 190°C. Fry the croquettes for 1 minute or until golden brown, then allow them to rest until warm before serving.

Kerth Gumbs

Having cut his teeth working in some of the UK's top kitchens, Kerth Gumbs is now combining the best of British ingredients with Caribbean flavours and influences from his Anguillan roots as head chef at the capital's Fenchurch.

Serves 8-10
3 hours, plus cooling time
Equipment: 12 hole muffin tin, electric whisk

Baileys custard
150g egg yolks
120g sugar
250g milk
250g whipping cream
1 vanilla pod
100ml Baileys

Parsnip cake
480g parsnips
370g flour
10g baking soda
8g baking powder
4g nutmeg
4g all spice
150g eggs
290ml vegetable oil
200g brown sugar
200g white sugar
100g shredded coconut, fresh or frozen
50g ginger, grated
3 pieces candied ginger, roughly chopped
oil for deep-frying

Chantilly cream
100ml double cream
15g sugar

Parsnip cake with salted Baileys custard

On the face of it parsnip cake sounds unusual, but it works just as well as (if not better than) carrot. The parsnip brings a slightly earthy flavour which balances the sweetness of the Baileys custard. These cakes are very sticky, so be sure to grease the tin well, and cool slightly before turning them out onto a wire rack.

Baileys custard Whisk the egg yolks with the sugar and 6g flaky sea salt.

Bring the milk, cream and vanilla pod to a bare simmer, then infuse for 5 minutes. Pour half of the hot milk mixture into the egg yolks and sugar and whisk to combine, then add the remaining milk mixture and whisk again.

Transfer the yolk mixture back into the pot, and cook over a low heat to 82°C, stirring constantly. Once at temperature, pass the custard through a fine chinois and cool before adding the Baileys.

Parsnip cake Preheat the oven to 170°C and grease the muffin tin very well.

Sift together the flour, baking soda, baking powder, spices and 10g salt. Peel the parsnips and set the skins aside for making parsnip skin crisps. Grate the peeled parsnips and then mix the grated parsnip with about a third of the flour mixture.

Whisk together the eggs, oil and sugar using an electric whisk until pale and well combined. Add the remaining flour mixture and mix on a low speed until combined. Add the parsnip mixture, coconut, fresh ginger and candied ginger and mix again. Use a spatula to scrape down the bowl, and check for any hidden lumps of flour.

Divide the batter between the cups of the muffin tin, making sure that each one is no more than three quarters full. Bake the muffins for around 20-25 minutes, or until a knife inserted into the centre comes out clean. Let the muffins cool in the tins for 10-15 minutes, then remove and set aside to cool on a wire rack.

To serve Whisk together the double cream and sugar for the Chantilly cream until they form soft peaks. Set aside.

Heat several centimetres of vegetable oil in a high-sided saucepan over medium-high heat until it reaches 150°C. Add the reserved parsnip skins and fry until golden and crisp, then remove from the oil and drain in paper towels. Season with salt.

Use the Chantilly cream to attach some parsnip crisps to the top of the cakes, and serve them with Baileys custard on the side.

Third generation sushi master Endo Kazutoshi has been turning heads with his impeccable sushi at London's Endo at The Rotunda since it opened in 2019 as a temple to his skill and mastery of Japanese omakase cookery (it received its first Michelin star less than a year later). He specialises in the centuries-old Edomae style, a technique particular to Tokyo, and his decades of experience in Japan are today intertwined with the UK's best seafood. Endo sees himself as a craftsman and is driven by a desire to constantly improve, a work ethic which, when matched with his incredible talent, has made him one of the most remarkable chefs in the country.

Endo Kazutoshi

Right: Endo creates precise,
elegant dishes for his
twenty-course omakase
menu.

Above: Endo puts the finishing
touches to his highly elevated
take on Gotō udon.

Serves 3-4 as a starter or side
30 minutes
Equipment: Pestle and mortar

160g white crab meat
25g brown crab meat
5g butter
pinch of white pepper
300g kombu dashi
3g kuzu

To serve
4 pinches mitsuba
4 teaspoons caviar
yuzu zest

Crab zosui

Zosui is a Japanese rice porridge cooked in a savoury dashi broth. In Endo Kazutoshi's luxurious version of this humble dish, crab meat replaces the rice, the delicate threads imitating broken down grains. It makes a delicious side dish as part of a larger Japanese meal.

Porridge Reserve 2 tablespoons of kombu dashi, then bring all the ingredients except the kuzu to a simmer and turn the heat to low.

Crush the kuzu powder with a pestle and mortar to get rid of any lumps, then whisk in the reserved kombu dashi to form a smooth slurry.

To serve Pour the slurry into the dish and cook until the zosui thickens. Transfer the zosui to small bowls and serve each garnished with a pinch of mitsuba, a little caviar and yuzu zest.

Serves 4
1 hour 30 minutes

100g Gotō udon

Egg sauce
1 egg

Nori sauce
20g nori powder
20g olive oil
20g sesame oil

Udon dashi
3g katsuobushi
25g light soy sauce
20g mirin
8g sugar

To serve
8g bottarga
truffle oil
nori powder
hana hojiso (shiso blossoms)
truffle salt
16 slices abalone

Gotō udon

Gotō udon is a regional type of udon from the Gotō islands, far off the coast of western Japan. The springy, chewy noodles are polished with camellia oil, and stretched by hand using a technique called teyori. Here Endo Kazutoshi serves them with bottarga, abalone and truffle, as well as a scattering of flowering shiso, or hana hojiso.

Egg sauce Cook the whole egg in a water bath at 65°C for 33 minutes. Alternatively, a little beaten raw egg can be stirred through each bowl to serve.

Nori sauce Mix all the ingredients together in a small bowl. Set aside.

Udon dashi The udon dashi has two components – a katsuobushi dashi and a kaeshi, or mixture of sugar, mirin and soy sauce.

To make the katsuobushi dashi, bring 600ml water to a simmer. Turn the heat to low and simmer the katsuobushi flakes for 1 minute. Remove from the heat and allow the katsuobushi flakes to steep for 90 seconds, then strain through a fine mesh sieve.

Combine the soy sauce, mirin and sugar, stirring until the sugar has dissolved. Mix 100g of the hot dashi with 11g of kaeshi and 0.5g salt. Set aside.

To serve Cook the Gotō udon in plenty of boiling water for 5 minutes or until tender. Drain the noodles and rinse well in cold water. Transfer to a bowl of cold water to chill the noodles.

Divide the noodles between four bowls. Add 18g udon dashi to each bowl. Top each one with 3g nori sauce, 6g egg sauce, 2g bottarga and a drop of truffle oil.

Add a dusting of nori powder, some hana hojiso and a pinch of truffle salt to each bowl, then top each one with four slices of abalone.

As chef director of the Cubitt House pub group, Ben Tish is committed to showing that pub food can go far beyond what people consider the traditional classics. Following years spent as Chef Director of the Salt Yard Group and then The Stafford Collection, he's now transforming the food offering of nine London pubs, giving each of their menus a distinct feel whilst also ensuring that his signature Mediterranean style shines through in every dish. Ben's food isn't about daring flavours or ultra-refined plating, it's about crowd-pleasing combinations and beautifully cooked produce and for that, there are few better.

Ben Tish

**Above: Ben tosses freshly
cooked pasta with thin discs
of courgette in the kitchen
at The Orange, Pimlico.**

Below top: Ben's Basque cheesecake is a stalwart of the dessert menus at his London pubs.

Below bottom: Ben uses a combination of green and yellow courgettes in his pasta dish to bring further colour to the plate.

Serves 4
40 minutes

200ml extra virgin olive oil
2 cloves garlic, crushed
2 medium courgettes, sliced into
thin discs
450g spaghetti or linguine
100g pecorino, finely grated
handful of mint leaves, roughly
chopped
grated zest of ½ lemon
1 tbsp pangrattato, or breadcrumbs
fried in oil
bottarga, to finish

Pasta with courgettes, mint, lemon and bottarga
This light Southern Italian pasta recipe from Ben Tish is quick to make and uses just a few core ingredients including courgettes, pecorino and garlic. Finished with crunchy fried breadcrumbs and a grating of bottarga for an added pop of colour and umami flavour, it's a wonderful illustration of how simple yet delicious a restaurant dish can be.

Courgettes Bring a large pan of salted water to the boil and heat a large sauté pan over medium heat. Add the olive oil – enough for shallow frying – and the garlic. Once the garlic begins to brown, add the courgette slices and fry until nicely golden brown.

Pasta Add the pasta to the boiling water and cook until al dente, 8-10 minutes.

When all the courgette slices are fried, take the pan off the heat and use a slotted spatula to transfer the slices to some paper towels to drain. Season well with salt and pepper.

When the pasta is cooked, transfer it to the courgette oil using tongs. Add a ladleful of pasta water. Put the pan back on the heat, and toss the pasta through the oil to coat.

To serve Sprinkle in some of the cheese and the mint, toss the pasta, then add the fried courgette slices, more cheese and the fried breadcrumbs and toss again. Grate over some bottarga to serve.

Serves 12-14
1 hour, plus cooling time
Equipment: 20 cm round
spring-form cake tin

Cheesecake
600g cream cheese
200g mascarpone
225g caster sugar
2 tbsp plain flour
200g sour cream
4 eggs
1 tsp vanilla extract

Cherries
200ml amontillado sherry
50g caster sugar
200g cherries, pitted

Basque cheesecake with cherries in amontillado

Hailing from Spain's Basque Country, this traditional baked cheesecake is cooked at a high heat to ensure it has a caramelised, slightly bitter top to cut through the creaminess below. Ben adds a further Spanish twist by serving it alongside boozy cherries macerated in amontillado sherry.

Cheesecake Preheat the oven to 250°C and place a rack in the centre of the oven.

Grease the cake tin generously with oil. Lay two large sheets of baking parchment on top of each other, then turn one of the sheets 45 degrees so that the corners form a star. Push the baking parchment into the tin, pressing it evenly around the bottom. There should be plenty of overhang, and don't worry about it being uneven.

Place the cream cheese, mascarpone and sugar into a bowl or stand mixer. Whisk together until smooth and creamy and the sugar has completely dissolved.

Add in the flour, sour cream, eggs, vanilla extract, and a pinch of sea salt. Mix again until you have a smooth mixture, and all the ingredients are fully incorporated.

Transfer the mixture to the tin, then knock the tin on the worktop to remove any air bubbles. Bake for 30-35 mins, or until the cake still has a good jiggle and the top is dark brown and well caramelised. It should be a deep mahogany – the bitterness contrasts with the sweetness and richness of the cake.

Once the cake is cooked, remove and cool at room temperature before transferring to the fridge to chill for 1 hour.

Cherries While the cake cooks, prepare the cherries. Simmer the sherry with the sugar for 2 minutes, then turn the heat down to very low and add the cherries. Cook for 2 minutes then remove from the heat and leave to macerate for 1 hour.

To serve Serve the cheesecake in generous slices with the cherries on the side.

Budgie Montoya

Budgie Montoya has dedicated his career to showing how vibrant Filipino cooking can be, yet he isn't bound by tradition. Combining influences of European kitchens, British produce and traditional flavours at his London concept Sarap, he's earned a reputation as one of the UK's most exciting chefs.

Serves 6-8
2 hours 30 minutes
Equipment: Steamer, stand mixer

Pork filling
vegetable oil, for frying
3 garlic cloves, minced
1 large onion, finely diced
500g pork shoulder, chopped into small pieces
1 tbsp hoisin sauce
1 tbsp soy sauce
3 tbsp oyster sauce
3 tbsp brown sugar

Siopao dough
7g instant yeast
500g plain flour
100g sugar
2 tbsp vegetable oil

Siopao asado

Siopao asado are Filipino steamed pork buns, often filled with sweet braised pork. Wrapping the pork buns neatly takes quite a bit of practice, so to start with just focus on making sure that the filling is completely sealed by the dough, so that no pork bursts out as the dough rises in the steamer.

Pork filling Heat a saucepan over medium-high heat, and add a splash of oil. Add the garlic and onion and sauté for around 10 minutes, or until softened and translucent. Add the pork, and fry until browned.

Add the hoisin sauce, soy sauce, oyster sauce, brown sugar, and 120ml water and turn the heat down to medium-low. Simmer the pork for about 1 hour 30 minutes, or until the sauce thickens and the pork is tender, adding another splash of water as needed.

Once the pork filling is tender, set aside to cool.

Siopao dough While the pork filling cools, make the dough. Bloom the yeast in 250ml warm water for 10-15 minutes. Whisk together the flour, sugar and 9g salt in the bowl of a stand mixer. Add the yeasty water and vegetable oil, and knead using a stand mixer with the dough hook attachment for 10-15 minutes, or until the dough becomes elastic and smooth. Cover the bowl with a damp tea towel and set aside until it doubles in size.

To serve Once the dough has risen, punch it down to release any air, and knead it again for 2-3 minutes. Divide the dough into 25 equal pieces.

Flatten each piece of dough into a circle, and add a spoonful of filling in the centre, then seal the siopao by pinching or pleating the edges together.

Place each siopao on a small square of baking parchment and let rest for another 10-15 minutes.

Steam the siopao for 15-20 minutes over high heat, or until the dough is cooked through.

Since taking it over in 2007, Stosie Madi has transformed The Parkers Arms in Lancashire into one of the most celebrated gastropubs in the country, famed in particular for its hearty home-made pies. The finest regional produce and rich terroir of the Trough of Bowland are honoured in a menu of modern British dishes with splashes of international influence, at times taken from Stosie's French and Lebanese heritage, Senegalese roots and Gambian upbringing. The end result is exciting, clever cooking which manages to feel both local and global at the same time.

Stosie Madi

Below: Fillets of gurnard are cooked on the grill to achieve perfectly crispy skin.

Right: Stosie runs the kitchen at The Parkers Arms almost entirely single-handedly to ensure that the pub's food is consistently excellent.

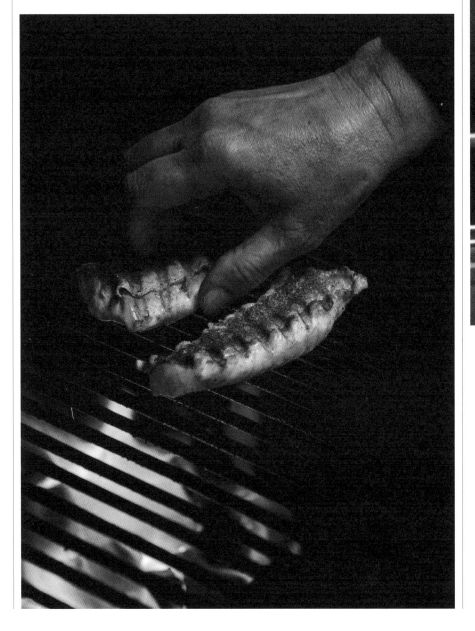

Right: Stosie's menu changes regularly to reflect the seasonal ingredients available locally, such as wild garlic in spring.

Serves 4
1 hour, plus overnight marinating and
pickling time
Equipment: Stick blender,
4 metal skewers, barbecue

Chicken brochette
25g fresh red jalapeno chilli paste
40g crunchy peanut butter
30g tamarind paste
30g fresh ginger paste
15g fresh garlic paste
50ml chicken jelly
10g brown sugar
20ml vegetable oil
20ml rice wine vinegar
600g chicken breast or skinless
boneless chicken thighs, cubed
80g roasted peanuts,
roughly chopped

Pickled daikon
250g daikon
5g sugar
50ml rice vinegar

Peanut and tamarind sauce
25g vegetable oil
15g fresh garlic paste
20g onion paste
15g fresh chilli paste
15g fresh ginger paste
50g tomato paste
200ml chicken stock
80g peanut butter
40g fresh tamarind paste
20g brown sugar

Fried wild garlic
a few wild garlic leaves
vegetable oil, for frying

Peanut-crusted chicken brochette, pickled daikon

Inspired by Stosie's love of Asian satay chicken and her memories of growing up on a peanut farm, this recipe combines a tangy tamarind-peanut sauce with peanut-crusted chicken and sharp pickled daikon. It makes a great starter or can be served with rice as a main.

Chicken brochette marinade Blend together all of the ingredients except for the chicken and roughly chopped peanuts. Add the paste to the chicken, and mix well. Leave to marinate overnight.

Pickled daikon Peel and thinly slice the daikon and toss with the sugar and 5g salt. Transfer to a colander and leave to strain for at least 2 hours. After this time, strain and transfer to a bowl, add the rice wine vinegar, toss well and marinate overnight.

Peanut and tamarind sauce Heat the oil in a pan, add the garlic, onion, fresh chilli, ginger and tomato pastes, and cook until fragrant and slightly softened. Add the chicken stock and mix well, then add the rest of the ingredients.

Blend with a stick blender until smooth, then cook over a low heat until the sauce is reduced and, ideally, the peanut oil breaks out from the sauce. Taste for seasoning and keep warm until ready to serve.

Chicken brochette Thread the marinated chicken onto skewers and prepare the barbecue for cooking the chicken.

Grill the chicken while constantly basting with the marinade, rotating constantly until tender – about 6 minutes. Once the chicken is cooked, roll each skewer in the chopped peanuts, mixing well to cover.

Fried wild garlic Heat 1 cm oil in a small frying pan and briefly fry the wild garlic leaves for 30 seconds or so, or until they crisp up. Drain on paper towels.

To serve Place a skewer on a plate, spoon a little warm sauce on the side and serve alongside the pickled daikon.

Serves 4
1 hour
Equipment: Barbecue, blender

4 large gurnard fillets, skin on and
very well pin boned
1 tbsp vegetable oil
2 tsp good quality curry powder

Crab sauce
1 × 500-600g whole crab
25ml vegetable oil
50g shallots, diced
50g garlic paste
1 tsp ground cumin
1 tsp ground fennel
1 tsp ground star anise
½ tsp ground cinnamon
50g carrot, grated
3 red chillies, sliced
50g coriander, chopped
10g fresh turmeric, grated
150ml coconut milk
60g tamarind paste
125ml anchovy garum or fish sauce
to taste

To serve
16 oyster leaves

Charcoal-grilled gurnard, curried crab sauce

Despite being both delicate and brilliantly meaty, gurnard remains a criminally underused fish in the UK. In this quick and simple recipe, Stosie crisps the gurnard fillets' skin over live fire before serving them alongside a silky crab sauce spiced with turmeric, fennel, coriander and chilli.

Crab sauce Preheat the oven to 180°C.

Steam the crab for 12 minutes, then transfer to a bowl to rest and collect the juices from the crab. Open up the crab and separate the white and brown meat.

Place the crab shells on an oven tray and brown in the oven until lightly toasted, then transfer to a large saucepan. Cover the shells with water and boil furiously for 10 minutes to get a light crab stock. Strain the stock, add the reserved crab juices and reduce it to 250ml over a high heat.

Transfer the stock to a blender, then add in the brown crab meat. Blend until smooth and set aside.

Sweat the shallots and garlic gently over low heat with the vegetable oil and dry spices. Add the carrot, chillies, coriander and turmeric and cook down slightly. Pour in the coconut milk, tamarind paste and garum or fish sauce, then cook for 20 minutes over a low heat. Add the crab stock and simmer for 15 minutes, then blend until smooth while hot and set aside.

Gurnard Thirty minutes before grilling, brush the fillets with the oil on both sides. Sprinkle the curry powder on the skin side only and season well with salt. Prepare a barbecue for cooking the fish.

To serve Stir the white crab meat into the crab sauce.

Grill the fish skin side down on the hot barbecue for 2 minutes, then flip and grill for 20-30 seconds longer.

Plate each portion of fish and serve with the sauce, oyster leaves and some sticky rice or noodles on the side.

Despite growing up eating Malaysian food, it wasn't until Abby Lee returned home during the pandemic in 2020 that she started learning more about the cuisine and cooking it for herself. She returned to London later that year and founded Mambow, a casual Malaysian open-kitchen restaurant in Peckham, where she's now making it her mission to introduce Londoners to the flavours of her childhood. In doing so, she's offering up some of the punchiest flavours in the capital, which, when combined with her modern approach to the cuisine, have seen Abby tipped as one of the country's brightest young talents.

Abby Lee

Below: Abby carefully stuffs
her bream with spicy sambal,
ready for deep frying.

**Above: Mambow is located
in a stall space within
the Peckham Market
development in south
east London.**

Serves 2
1 hour 30 minutes
Equipment: Steamer,
food processor

Curry paste
60g lemongrass, bottom half thinly
sliced and tops saved for flavouring
other dishes
35g galangal, thinly sliced
10g coriander seeds
30g dried Kashmiri chilli, boiled
for 3 minutes until softened
then strained
350g white onion, roughly chopped
45g ginger, roughly chopped
40g Thai soybean paste, optional
4g ground turmeric

Pineapple curry
vegetable oil, for cooking
20g granulated sugar
¼ pineapple, cut into 2 cm triangles
8 lime leaves, torn into pieces
70g tamarind concentrate

Chive dumplings
200g garlic chives, cut into
1 cm pieces
10g granulated sugar
20g neutral oil
1g ground white pepper
100g rice flour
100g tapioca starch

Tangy pineapple curry and chive dumplings

This pineapple curry from Abby Lee is served with chewy deep-fried chive dumplings. The pineapple curry's deep flavour comes from a slow-cooked rempah that is full of fresh aromatics like lemongrass and galangal. It's really important to properly cook down the rempah, so be patient and keep cooking it until it's fully browned.

Curry paste Combine all the paste ingredients except the turmeric, salt and sugar in a food processor. Blend until smooth, then transfer to a bowl and mix in the turmeric until combined.

Pineapple curry Add some oil to a wok or saucepan until it is 0.5 cm deep. Add the curry paste and fry it over medium heat until the oil has separated – this can take 20-30 minutes.

Stir regularly, and turn the heat to low if the paste starts to stick to the bottom of the pan. Once the paste is ready, add 18g fine sea salt and the sugar and let it caramelise for another 2-3 minutes. Add the pineapple, 400g water and 6 lime leaves, saving the remainder for garnish.

Turn the heat down to low and let the curry simmer on low heat for 20 minutes. This is not a super loose curry; it should reduce down into a thick sauce. Add the tamarind, and then taste and adjust the seasoning. Every pineapple will have a different level of sweetness, so add tamarind to make it more tart if needed.

Chive dumplings Mix the garlic chives, 5g fine sea salt, sugar, white pepper and oil. Set aside to marinade for 20 minutes.

Whisk together the rice flour, tapioca starch, and 240g water until you have a smooth batter. Add the batter to a pan, and continuously stir on a low heat until the mixture forms a thick paste – it should not move much when you use a spatula to push it to the side. If lumps start forming during the cooking process, use a whisk to get rid of them as much as you can.

At the same time, heat up a steamer and find a small container for steaming the dumplings in. The batter should be 3 cm deep so any heatproof dish over that height will work well.

Mix the thickened batter with the chive mixture until combined. Oil the dish of your choice, then line the bottom with baking parchment. Pour the mixture into the dish, spreading very evenly to a height of 3 cm. You can use a piece of baking parchment to press down the top to get rid of any air bubbles in the batter.

Steam the dumplings for 15 minutes on high heat. Test them using a toothpick – there should be some batter on the toothpick but it shouldn't be sticky. Let the dumplings cool for at least 30 minutes before cutting them into squares.

Deep-fry the dumplings at 175°C until golden brown.

To serve Very thinly slice the remaining lime leaves. Warm up the pineapple curry, and serve with the fried chive dumplings on top, the lime leaves and lime wedges.

Serves 2 with other dishes
2 hours
Equipment: Blender

1 × 400-550g whole sea bream,
scaled but not gutted
vegetable oil for deep-frying and for
frying the sambal
2 lime wedges, to serve

Sambal
320g red onion, roughly chopped
320g long red chillies, roughly
chopped
25g dried Kashmiri chilli, boiled
for 3 minutes until softened
then strained
280g lemongrass, bottom half thinly
sliced and tops saved for flavouring
other dishes
20g belacan
6g ground turmeric
50g tamarind concentrate
60g granulated sugar

Kerabu
60g green mango, sliced into 2 mm
strips but not peeled
30g green apple, sliced into
2 mm strips
30g beansprouts
10g red onion, thinly sliced
5g red chilli, sliced into 2 mm strips
2 sprigs of mint, thinly sliced
1 sprig of Vietnamese mint or
coriander, thinly sliced

Kerabu dressing
12g fish sauce (preferably Red
Boat fish sauce)
25g calamansi or lime juice
10g granulated sugar
1 red birds eye chilli, thinly sliced

Rempah fish and green mango kerabu

This Nyonya fish dish from Abby Lee is best made with gilthead bream, but can be made with any sea bream. Make sure to buy a whole fish that is descaled but not gutted since the guts are removed from the head. This recipe also makes more sambal than is needed, but it will keep for about two weeks in the fridge.

Sambal Blend the red onion, red chilli, dried chilli, lemongrass and belacan in a food processor – a slightly rough texture is fine. Transfer to a bowl and mix in the turmeric.

Heat 1 cm of oil in a saucepan over medium heat. Cook the paste until the oil has separated and the sambal has a drier texture. This can take up to 30 minutes, so stir regularly. If the bottom starts to stick, reduce the heat to medium-low.

Add the tamarind, 15g fine sea salt and sugar. Let caramelise for another 2-3 minutes.

Prep the bream Use scissors to cut off the bream's gills, then gut the fish and clean the bloodline. Rinse the fish and dry well.

Make a slit at the back of the fish, starting from the back of the head and going down to the middle. Keep running your knife through to open the fish internally as if you are filleting but keeping it intact. Repeat on the other side.

Kerabu Mix all the kerabu ingredients in a bowl. Prepare the dressing by mixing all the ingredients well until all the sugar has been dissolved. Add a few tablespoons of dressing at a time to the kerabu, tasting as you go. There should be some leftover dressing for other salads. Leave the salad to marinate for 5-10 minutes

Stuffing and frying the fish Heat a few inches of oil for deep-frying the fish to 180°C in a high-sided saucepan.

Weigh out 250g of the cooked sambal. Using a spoon, stuff the sambal into both pockets of the bream, ensure you are getting all the way down to the stomach. Keep pushing and spreading it around.

Deep-fry the stuffed fish for 4-6 minutes depending if you are on the 400g or 550g end of the weight of the fish. It should be completely submerged in the oil.

To serve Serve the fish with lime wedges and green mango kerabu on top or on the side.

Andrew Gravett

Pastry has always been Andrew Gravett's focus in the kitchen, and as executive pastry chef at The Langham Hotel in London, he's able to showcase his incredible talent for creating everything from pies and breads to elaborate desserts and cakes.

Serves 4
3 hours
Equipment: 8 cm round cutter, piping bags, stick blender

Rice pudding cream
350g milk
90g honey
5g cinnamon
50g rice, rinsed and drained

Almond sablé
90g unsalted butter, softened
70g icing sugar
35g egg, beaten
20g ground almonds
185g plain flour

Light almond cream
65g ground almonds
60g caster sugar
20g cornflour
50g butter, softened
40g egg
40g whipping cream

Granny Smith compote
700g Granny Smith apples, peeled, cored and finely chopped
5g fruit pectin
50g sugar
2g citric acid

To serve
5 Granny Smith apples, peeled
100g sugar
100g whipping cream

Apple almond tart

This pretty tart brings together the nostalgic flavours of zingy Granny Smith apples, sweet and creamy rice pudding and fragrant ground almonds. The compote, almond cream, sablé and rice pudding can all be made in advance.

Rice pudding cream Add the milk, honey and cinnamon to a saucepan and bring to the boil. Add the rice, and cook for 30 minutes, or until soft and thickened. Set aside to cool.

Almond sablé Beat together the softened butter, icing sugar, ground almonds and egg until smooth. Add the flour and a pinch of salt, and beat again until just combined.

Roll the dough out between 2 sheets of baking parchment until it's 3 mm thick. Cut out the dough using an 8 cm cutter, and transfer to the freezer for 15 minutes on a baking parchment-lined tray.

Preheat the oven to 160°C.

Bake the sablé on a baking parchment-lined tray for 12-15 minutes, until golden. Set aside.

Light almond cream Preheat the oven to 170°C.

Combine the ground almonds, a pinch of salt and the caster sugar, then sieve in the cornflour. Add the butter, cream and egg, then beat until fully incorporated. Transfer to a piping bag.

Pipe an even layer of almond cream onto the sablé. Bake for 15-20 minutes, or until lightly browned. Set aside to cool.

Granny Smith compote Cook the chopped apple over a medium heat in a covered pan until softened, about 15 minutes. Weigh out 500g of cooked apple purée.

Add the sugar and pectin to the 500g of apple purée and cook for another 2 minutes or so. Blend until smooth with a stick blender, then add the citric acid. Transfer to a piping bag.

Pipe an even layer of compote over the sablé, then chill.

Garnish Cut a 3 cm wide ring from the middle of the apple and use a peeler to cut ribbons. You will need to press very firmly.

Dissolve the sugar in 200ml water over a medium heat. Add the apple slices and poach for a couple of minutes, or until translucent. Remove from the syrup and set aside.

To serve Whip the cream to soft peaks. Weigh out 150g of the cooled rice pudding and fold it into the cream.

Garnish each tart with apple ribbons, trying to get as much volume as possible. Serve with the rice pudding cream.

Lisa Goodwin-Allen draws inspiration from the landscapes around her, taking local produce and elevating it in plates which are led by the seasons. Her playful style means she isn't afraid to take treasured Lancastrian dishes and reimagine them, adding her own twists. Lisa first became head chef of the Michelin-starred Northcote in Lancashire at twenty-three, having joined as a demi chef de partie only three years before. Today, she remains its executive chef, is a familiar face on our TV screens and has ventured into the capital with The Game Bird and The American Bar at hotel The Stafford. Lisa has long been at the helm of British food and remains one of Britain's most exciting chefs.

Lisa Goodwin-Allen

Left: Lisa pipes vanilla cream onto caramelised puff pastry for her mille feuille dessert.

Above: The vanilla cream layer is delicately balanced on top of piped chocolate curd for a refined finish.

Serves 4

3 hours, plus time for the herb oil to freeze overnight

Equipment: Stand mixer or electric whisk, blender

4 × 170g pieces of aged venison loin
oil, for cooking

Tarragon oil
50g tarragon
200ml rapeseed oil
Ice water

Hazelnut crust
150g salted butter, room temperature
100g marrow, removed from the bone
80g brioche, blitzed into crumbs
50g lilliput capers
50g hazelnuts, toasted and crushed
2 tsp chopped chives

Red wine sauce
oil, for cooking
1 medium shallot, roughly chopped
1 small clove of garlic, finely chopped
1 sprig thyme, torn
200ml red wine
250ml chicken stock
250ml beef stock

Bourguignon sauce
30g olive oil
100g onion, diced
100g smoked pancetta, diced
100g mushrooms, diced
1½ tsp roast garlic
dash of red verjus
1 tsp chopped parsley
1 tablespoon lilliput capers

Mushroom purée
50g butter
500g white mushrooms, thinly sliced
300g whipping cream

Hazelnut-crusted aged venison, smoked pancetta and mushroom bourguignon

Lisa's refined take on a classic combination of ingredients combines hazelnut-crusted venison with a rich bourguignon sauce and creamy mushroom purée. Lisa recommends using Otoñol Rioja in the sauce.

Tarragon oil Heat the rapeseed oil to 70°C and prepare a bowl of ice water. Place the tarragon in a blender and blend with the hot oil until smooth (do this in batches if needed). Make sure there is a way for steam to escape from the blender, and cover the steam vent with a tea towel to protect your hands.

Pour the oil into a bowl, then set it over the bowl of ice water. Chill the herb oil, then freeze overnight.

The next day, the oil will have separated from the solids. Pour off the green oil into a new container and discard the solids.

Hazelnut crust Combine the butter and marrow in a stand mixer and beat until soft and pale. Add the remaining ingredients and mix well.

Spread the mixture between 2 sheets of baking parchment to a 1 cm thickness. Place on a tray and transfer to the freezer to set.

Red wine sauce Add a little oil to a saucepan over medium heat. Add the shallot and cover. Cook for 2-3 minutes until softened, then remove the lid and cook for 5- 8 minutes until caramelised.

Add the garlic, thyme and red wine. Turn the heat up to high and reduce the red wine sauce by 3/4, or until the liquid coats the shallots. Add the chicken and beef stock, then reduce over high heat until it coats the back of a spoon. Pass through a fine sieve.

Bourguignon sauce Heat a pan over medium heat, then add the olive oil. Once hot, add the onion, pancetta, mushrooms and garlic and cook for 2-3 minutes. Add the verjus and cook for 1-2 minutes, or until the verjus has mostly evaporated. Add 250g of the red wine sauce and simmer for 2-3 minutes, until slightly reduced. Add the parsley and capers, mix and season if needed.

Mushroom purée Melt the butter in a large pan over medium heat. Add the mushrooms, season with salt, then cover and cook the mushrooms for 4-5 minutes. Remove the lid, then reduce any liquid the mushrooms have released, stirring frequently.

Add the cream and simmer until reduced by half. Transfer to a blender until smooth, then pass through a fine sieve. Season.

To serve Preheat the oven to 150°C.

Season the venison well with salt and pepper and heat a dash of oil in a pan. Sear the venison loins on all sides until nicely caramelised. Remove from the pan and place on an oven tray.

Cut out rounds of the hazelnut crust that are roughly the same size as the venison. Place a round on each fillet and roast for 10-12 minutes for medium-rare venison. Remove the fillets from the oven and transfer to a wire rack to rest for 4-5 minutes.

Add a spoonful of bourguignon sauce to each plate, then drizzle with tarragon oil. Cut the sides off the venison and place on top. Spoon some mushroom purée on the side and serve.

Serves 4
2 hours 30 minutes, plus time for the ice cream to chill and curd to set
Equipment: Blowtorch, stick blender, ice cream maker

Salted milk ice cream
1 litre milk
85g glucose
85g milk powder
3g stabiliser
85g sugar

Chocolate curd
200g milk
150g egg yolk
100g sugar
300g Valrhona Jivara 40% milk chocolate, roughly chopped
5 gelatine leaves, soaked in ice water
550g cream

Vanilla cream
600ml milk
2 vanilla pods
250g egg yolk
100g caster sugar
90g plain flour
200g whipping cream
ice water

Caramelised puff pastry
300g puff pastry
golden caster sugar, as needed

Valrhona chocolate mille-feuille, salted milk ice cream

Caramelised puff pastry is layered with fragrant vanilla cream and a 40% milk chocolate curd in this elegant yet crowd-pleasing mille feuille. Lisa serves hers with tempered chocolate shards.

Salted milk ice cream Bring the milk and glucose to a simmer in a pan, whisking to dissolve the glucose. Mix together the milk powder, stabiliser and sugar.

Add the powders to the milk mixture and whisk until combined. Boil for 2 minutes, then remove from the heat. Add 5g sea salt and blend with a stick blender.

Pass through a fine sieve and chill in the fridge. Once cool, churn in an ice cream maker and transfer to the freezer to firm up.

Chocolate curd Bring the milk to a bare simmer over medium heat. Whisk together the yolks and sugar until thick and pale. Pour the milk over the yolks in a steady stream, whisking constantly. Transfer back into a pan and cook to 82°C.

Transfer the chocolate to a bowl, pour the custard over and add the gelatine. Allow to sit for 1 minute then whisk to emulsify, starting at the centre of the bowl and working outwards.

Very lightly whip the cream, then fold it into the chocolate emulsion. Transfer to a container and set in the fridge for a minimum of 2 hours. Once set, gently whisk the chocolate curd and transfer to a piping bag. Set aside until ready to assemble.

Vanilla cream Bring the milk and vanilla to a boil over medium heat. Whisk together the egg yolks, sugar and flour in a bowl until well combined.

Once the milk has begun to bubble, pour it into the egg mixture while whisking constantly to ensure that the hot milk does not scramble the egg yolk and the flour is completely incorporated.

Strain through a fine sieve, then transfer back to the pan. Cook on medium heat for 10 minutes, whisking constantly until thickened.

Transfer the vanilla cream to a bowl set over a bowl of ice water. Lightly whip the cream then fold through the cooled custard. Transfer to the fridge to set. Once set, transfer to a piping bag.

Caramelised puff pastry Preheat the oven to 180°C.

Roll out the puff pastry to 2 mm thickness and cut two 25 cm × 10 cm rectangles of pastry.

Place the rectangles on a lined baking tray, then place another piece of baking parchment and another tray on top. Bake 15- 20 minutes, until golden.

Remove from the oven and transfer to a chopping board. Use a serrated knife to cut each sheet into 8 even rectangles. Dust sugar over the top of each of the 8 pieces, then use a blowtorch to caramelise the sugar.

To serve Pipe an even layer of chocolate curd over 4 rectangles of pastry, and a layer of vanilla cream over the remaining four. Top each chocolate layer with a vanilla layer, and serve the mille-feuille with the ice cream.

Taking home the title at just twenty-six, Steven Edwards is one of the youngest winners in MasterChef: The Professionals history, a triumph which was testament to his ambitious and creative spirit. In 2017, he opened his first restaurant etch. in Hove, which has since been joined by Steven Edwards Riverhouse in Richmond. His accomplished modern British cookery centres around using just a couple of main ingredients in every dish and then enhancing them using a combination of herbs, sauces and technique. His menu is truly ever-changing, evolving throughout the year and giving his loyal diners a reason to come back again and again.

Steven Edwards

Above: Steven prepares a dish of lamb rump and salsify in the kitchen of his award-winning restaurant, etch.

Below: Coriander leaves are used to give the ice cream its bright green colour. Steven serves a quenelle on top of his honey and pear cake.

Serves 6
3 hours
Equipment: 20 mm round cutter, blender

Lamb
3 x 230g lamb rumps, square cut
oil, for cooking

Lamb sauce
200g onions, peeled and sliced
400ml white wine
500ml veal stock
500ml lamb stock
1 green pepper, sliced

Salsify
12 sticks of salsify
1 lemon, juiced
200g butter, plus 50g melted butter for the sauce
150g double cream
vegetable oil, for deep-frying

To serve
sorrel leaves

Slow-cooked lamb rump with salsify, salsify purée and salsify crisps

This recipe is a perfect example of Steven's two-ingredient approach. Salsify is made into a purée, deep-fried to make crisps, and also pan-fried in butter, providing a range of different textures to accompany the rare roasted rump.

Lamb Bring 2 litres water and 140g table salt to a boil, stirring to dissolve the salt completely. Set the brine aside, and, once cool, transfer to the fridge to thoroughly chill.

Remove any excess fat or skin from the rump, leaving a layer on top. Add to the brine and transfer to the fridge for 2 hours.

Lamb sauce Add the onions to a dry pan and cook until caramelised and sticky, stirring constantly, 30-40 minutes. Add the wine to deglaze the pan, using a spoon to scrape up any bits, then simmer until reduced by half. Add both stocks and bring to a simmer, then turn the heat down to low. Simmer gently for 1 hour.

Pass the sauce through a fine sieve, then return to the pan. Add the green pepper and reduce over high heat until the sauce coats the back of a spoon. Strain through a fine sieve or chinois.

Salsify Wash the salsify thoroughly, then peel and add to a bowl of water along with the lemon juice.

Take two sticks of salsify and peel them into ribbons with a vegetable peeler, then season lightly with flaky sea salt. Set aside to soften for 1 hour.

Cut the remaining salsify sticks into three pieces. Add to a saucepan with the butter and 200g water. Bring to a simmer then turn down to low and cook for 10-12 minutes or until just tender. Take 12 pieces of salsify out of the pan and set aside.

Continue to cook the rest of the salsify for 10-15 minutes or until very soft. Transfer to a blender with the melted butter and double cream. Blend until smooth and set aside.

Once the salsify ribbons have salted, heat several centimetres of vegetable oil to 170°C. Wash the ribbons under cold water very well, then squeeze as dry as you can. Pat dry very thoroughly.

Deep-fry the ribbons until hot and crispy.

To serve Preheat the oven to 180°C.

Wash the brined lamb under cold water and pat dry. Heat a frying pan with a dash of oil. Add the rumps and brown them on all sides, rendering down the fat on top of the rumps. Remove the rumps from the pan, reserving the pan, and transfer to an oven tray.

Roast the rumps in the oven for 12-15 minutes or until the core temperature reaches 40°C. Slice each rump into four pieces.

Cook the reserved, tender sticks of salsify in the pan with the rendered lamb fat until golden all over.

Cut out small circles from the sorrel leaves.

Add two pieces of the browned salsify to each plate, along with a tablespoon of purée and some salsify crisps. Lay two pieces of lamb rump on top of the golden salsify, then finish with some lamb sauce and the sorrel leaves.

Serves 6
3 hours 30 minutes, plus time
for the ice cream to chill
Equipment: Muffin tin, small round
cutter, medium round cutter,
ice cream maker

Coriander ice cream
100g coriander, leaves picked
and tough stems discarded
250ml milk
250ml double cream
5 egg yolks
90g caster sugar
ice water

Honey cake
100g butter
140g icing sugar
50g ground almonds
7g baking powder
50g plain flour
170g egg whites
15g honey

Roasted pear purée
6 Williams pears, peeled
and quartered

Poached pear
6 Williams pears
150g caster sugar
200ml white wine

**White chocolate and
bee pollen tuile**
180g fondant
80g glucose
80g white chocolate,
roughly chopped
2g bee pollen

To serve
coriander cress or sprigs
of coriander

Honey cake with poached pear compote and coriander ice cream

While it may look simple, a number of different processes combine to create this beautiful dessert. A vibrant herb ice cream and delicate white chocolate and bee pollen tuile sit atop the honey cake, which is filled with perfumed pear compote.

Coriander ice cream Blanch the coriander for 30 seconds, then transfer to an ice bath. Once cool, squeeze dry.

Heat the milk and cream to a bare simmer. Whisk the yolks and caster sugar together until pale. Pour the warm cream and milk mixture over the yolks in a steady stream, whisking constantly.

Cook the mixture over low heat, whisking, to 82°C. Chill for several hours, ideally overnight.

Add the coriander and blitz until smooth. Churn in an ice maker and transfer to the freezer to firm up.

Honey cake Brown the butter over low heat. Transfer to a bowl and cool. Grease the muffin tin and preheat the oven to 160°C.

Whisk together the icing sugar, almonds, baking powder and plain flour. Whisk in the egg whites and honey, then the brown butter. Divide between 6 muffin tin holes, each with ~75g batter.

Cook 25-30 minutes, until golden. Cool the cakes in the tin for 5 minutes, then remove and cool completely on a wire rack.

Cut a hole in the middle of each cake. Crumble the cut outs into crumbs and bake for 5-10 minutes to make the crumb.

Roasted pear purée Turn the oven up to 180°C and roast the pears for 45 minutes until dark brown and sticky. Blend to a purée then pass through a fine sieve.

Poached pear Bring the sugar, 500ml water and wine to a simmer. Poach the pears gently for 1 hour. Drain, cool, then dice.

Mix the diced pears with the roasted pear purée at a ratio of one part purée to 2 parts diced pears.

White chocolate and bee pollen tuile Heat the fondant and glucose to 155°C in a high-sided heavy saucepan. Remove from the heat and very carefully stir in the chocolate. Pour onto a lined tray. Set aside to harden.

Preheat the oven to 220°C, no fan.

Blitz the tuile to a powder and sieve onto a tray in a thin, even layer. Press a round cutter into it to make circular tuiles.

Bake for 4-6 minutes until the powder has joined back together. Remove from the oven and sprinkle quickly with pollen. Set aside to cool, then remove from the tray.

To serve When ready to serve, gently reheat the honey cake at a low heat in the oven, and warm up some of the compote in a saucepan. Take the ice cream out of the freezer to soften.

Fill each warm honey cake with the compote, and sprinkle the compote with some honey cake crumbs. Top the cake with a scoop or rocher of coriander ice cream, a bee pollen tuile and the coriander cress.

Index

Right: Pip Lacey carefully pours her crème caramel mixture into foil moulds filled with a dark muscovado caramel.

First published in the UK in 2023 by GreatBritishChefs and Clearview Books

Photographs and text
© 2023 GreatBritishChefs/Food Publishing (Books) Limited

Compilation copyright
© 2023 GreatBritishChefs/Food Publishing (Books) Limited

ISBN 978-1908337-726

Editor: Henry Coldstream
Creative Director: Helen Graves
Design Direction: Esterson Associates
Art Director: Holly Catford
Photography: Andrew Hayes-Watkins
Recipe Editor: Esme Curtis
Copywriter: Lauren Fitchett
Production: Rosanna Dickinson

Printed and bound in Croatia

A CIP record of this book is available from the British Library.